"This dynamic fresh approach to small group ministries breaks exciting new ground as it identifies the underlying principles of helping people grow spiritually in and through small groups. Breaking from more rigidly structured programmatic models, this people-centered developmental approach allows churches of all sizes to consider diverse forms and patterns of group life while it clearly addresses such key issues as purpose, atmosphere, growth, outreach, life cycles, leadership, and organizational dynamics. Small group planning teams, leaders, pastors, as well as laypeople wanting to reach out to those around them, will find it a stimulating and thorough guide. I wholeheartedly recommend it."

—The Rev. Dr. Roberta Hestenes
   International Minister for World Vision International
   and author of *Using the Bible in Groups* and
   From Committees to Community

Bethany House Publishers
Books Coauthored by David Stark

Growing People Through Small Groups *

LifeDirections †

LifeKeys ‡

LifeKeys Discovery Workbook ‡

LifeKeys Leadership Resource ‡

*with Betty Veldman Wieland   †with Jane Kise   ‡with Jane Kise and Sandra Krebs Hirsh

GROWING PEOPLE

THROUGH

SMALL GROUPS

David Stark
Betty Veldman Wieland

BETHANY HOUSE PUBLISHERS
Minneapolis, Minnesota

Published by Bethany House Publishers
11400 Hampshire Avenue South
Bloomington, Minnesota 55438
www.bethanyhouse.com

Bethany House Publishers is a Division of
Baker Book House Company, Grand Rapids, Michigan.

Printed in the United States of America

Library of Congress Cataloging-in-Publication Data

Stark, David, 1955-
    Growing people through small groups / by David Stark and Betty Veldman Wieland.
       p. cm.
    Includes bibliographical references.
    ISBN 0-7642-2912-5
    1. Church group work. 2. Small groups—Religious aspects—Christianity. I. Wieland,
Betty Veldman. II. Title.
    BV652.2.S73   2004
    253'.7—dc22   2004002191

DAVID STARK is the director of Changing Church through Prince of Peace Lutheran Church in Burnsville, Minnesota. The founder and director of training for Church Innovations, he has led dozens of workshops and seminars throughout the United States and has developed masters for small groups that are used by churches from a variety of denominations. David holds an M.Div. and has published a number of resources, including the LifeKeys books, for groups. He lives in Minnesota with his wife and two sons.

BETTY VELDMAN WIELAND was introduced to small groups through a women's Bible study. The experience ignited her passion for God's Word and led her to leadership positions in Christian Reformed Home Missions' small group ministry. Betty has two adult sons and she and her husband live in Michigan.

TABLE OF CONTENTS

Introduction 9

CHAPTER 1: Be Rooted in God's Will 15

CHAPTER 2: Grow People, Not Programs 23

CHAPTER 3: Create Atmospheres for a Diverse Set of People ... 41

CHAPTER 4: People Develop in Stages
PART ONE: Spiritual Development 61

CHAPTER 5: People Develop in Stages
PART TWO: Principles for Spiritual Development ... 71

CHAPTER 6: Grow What's Blooming 89

CHAPTER 7: Nurture What's Growing.................... 107

CHAPTER 8: Transplant What Needs Room to Grow 125

CHAPTER 9: The Leader Is a Gardener 139

CHAPTER 10: The Leader as Shepherd 159

Afterword 173

Resources 175

INTRODUCTION

I (David) remember the first time I attended a Leadership Network-sponsored event. I was a pastor in charge of the small-group ministry in my church; it was the late 1980s, and we all gathered from churches throughout the United States. At that point I was also working part time for Serendipity House, and many of us had spent time with Lyman Coleman, Serendipity's founder as well as one of the leaders of the small-group movement. I recall being fascinated by each story, every one of them different but containing threads of similarity among my counterparts in various congregations. Throughout the entire weekend, we were developing a strong bond of solidarity with one another and learning the important work of building transformational community within congregations.

In the early afternoon on the second day, however, our facilitator guided us through an exercise I'll never forget. He asked us to move to the south side of the room if we believed that small-group ministry requires a large amount of directive, supervisory leadership in order to succeed; he asked us to move to the north side of the room if we believed that small-group ministry needs more empowering, supportive leadership. He gave us the caveat that small-group ministry obviously needs some of both—the question was, Which type of leadership is *predominately* needed in order for us to succeed as small-group pastors? The room was almost equally divided between these two camps. We had a two-hour-long discussion, back and forth, about which perspective is right.

As I've walked with the small-group movement for parts of three decades, I've realized how important this essential difference has become. Many systems of small-group ministry are fundamentally run on a *mechanistic* model of organization, where control and compliance are the real outcomes. Conversely, many systems (and I would include ours in this camp) are fundamentally run on an *organic* understanding of organization, where trust and support are the real outcomes. If we have any single bias in this book, it's that true transformation isn't about conformity to anyone's standard—creating a trust-filled, supportive atmosphere opens the door for the Holy Spirit to transform people's lives from the inside out. Yes, there are advantages and challenges to both ways of operating a small-group ministry. For us, however, the most important question becomes, How do we help people to grow? It's our strong thesis that the Spirit works best in the context of freedom within boundaries of accountability.

At the writing of this book, we are seeing this same question being played out on a societal level, albeit not always within the context of specifically Christian community. On the one hand, Robert Putnam has argued, in *Bowling Alone: The Collapse and Revival of American Community,* that the collective value of social networking ("social capital") is dropping dramatically in America today—that formal associations are having a harder and harder time obtaining and maintaining members (including the mainline denominations). Serving as a counterpoint is Ethan Watters' work *Urban Tribes,* where he argues that below the radar screen of formal membership in organizations is a whole generation that is organically connecting in complex, interwoven networks of community, very much alive and well. As he puts it:

Sometimes they (the tribes) were even hard to see from the inside. At least a dozen people wrote to say that they hadn't even perceived their own tribe until they heard me describing mine. Was it possible that a group could grow so organically in the lives of its members that it could have escaped their own notice?

In order to win this generation to Christ, we need to understand that these "tribes," at least within their friendships and other connections, are operating very much like the body of Christ as described in the New Testament—supporting, helping, protecting, celebrating one another. I'm *not* saying that all of these groups operate on the basis of Jesus Christ being Lord, or that they are unilaterally (in any way) to be considered Christian. What I *am* saying is that the church of the future must respond to these communities by offering organic relational structures based on commitment to Jesus, living out our calling as Christians in the world. In other words, we believe that organic small-group systems are not only more effective in facilitating genuine transformation, but that they will also build a strong bridge for the evangelization and discipleship of the next generation.

For fifteen years, I (Betty) watched God transform women's lives through Coffee Break, a church-based, inductive Bible-study program for newcomers to the Word. Coffee Break was my introduction to small groups, and in that setting of women loving women and letting Scripture speak for itself, many women committed their lives to Jesus Christ for the very first time. Others renewed their faith commitment, becoming passionate about sharing their faith—and their lives—with others. I became a believer in the power of a small group.

In 1995, after six years as International Director of Coffee Break, I was challenged to think more broadly. What would it look like to have small groups throughout the whole church, rather than only as a Bible study for women? How could small groups be part of the outreach strategy for an entire denomination? "Dream big," I was urged, with no more guidance than "You figure it out" (and, thankfully, the promise of prayers for my work, as well as the time, space, and resources to do the job).

That challenge led to more questions. What kind of small-group strategy would reach beyond the walls of the church building? How could we engage men in small groups? How could small groups connect with non-Christians from the community who are not yet ready for a Bible study? What would it take to involve a whole church in small groups, from those on the fringes, disconnected from body life, to those desiring to delve deeply into spiritual disciplines with other committed Christians—from spiritual seekers to those hungry for authentic community with other believers?

To say it in popular terms, I needed to think outside the box and, if possible, not reinvent the wheel. I devoured books on small groups, attended conferences, talked with small-group leaders, attended training, and explored many wonderful models. Several were God-blessed small-group models with passionate leaders, and all of them worked in certain settings. In the end I became convinced of one thing: There is no one-size-fits-all small-group model for an entire denomination.

There was a time when such a model may have worked, because churches within denominations once tended to look very much alike. However, the diversity of our North American culture has, particularly in the past half-century, spilled over into the church as well. For instance, the denomination I am a part of, the Christian Reformed Church in North America (CRCNA), has moved beyond her Dutch heritage and embraced believers of many other ethnic roots. Though all the churches in the CRCNA espouse the same creeds, individual churches within the denomination increasingly reflect their members' cultural diversity. Worship is one example: Some still hold to a traditional, classical, highly liturgical style; some prefer a more contemporary style, with bands, praise teams, and up-to-date music; still others try to find the blend that will please a variety of palates. Just as services differ widely from congregation to congregation, small-group ministries will vary from church to church.

After digesting so much small-group input, I ended right where I started—Coffee Break. I and a team of co-workers (regional small-group representatives from across the U.S. and Canada) took a hard look at what made Coffee Break successful in a wide variety of churches; listing these factors, or principles, seemed like a logical place to begin.

Then, at a Leadership Network-sponsored forum for small-group consultants, I found the connection I'd been seeking. It was there that I met David Stark, a pastor and small-group consultant, and I knew that his strategy—a principle-based approach—was the fit I'd been seeking. Dave's subsequent meeting with our team of small-group representatives affirmed the compatibility, and God opened doors for us to work together.

Principle-based small-group ministry works well in a wide variety of settings because, among other reasons, it presumes the diversity of churches and denominations. Its guiding principles have challenged churches to move beyond one-size-fits-all models, freeing them to dream God's dreams for their small-group ministries. It has re-ignited the passion and energy of those who had become discouraged from trying to implement models that didn't quite fit. It has also released people into small-group leadership based on their gifts and motivations.

Principle-based small groups are effective because they honor God's desire for His church and they honor the diversity of the people He created. These are the keys to effective small groups. May you, likewise, discover the freedom and freshness of growing people in ways that God intended.

CHAPTER ONE:

BE ROOTED IN GOD'S WILL

Mary was elated. She was on her way home after conducting a small-group workshop in a small but vibrant Salt Lake City church, and she could still feel the excitement of the on-fire leadership group. They "got it," meaning they understood the concept of principle-based small groups and how it fit with their already-clear vision of God's call for their church. She couldn't wait to share their passion—and her own.

The dedicated Christians in this tiny church had told Mary story after story of how God was using them to reach Mormons with the gospel of grace through Jesus. Led by an evangelist who was fervent about reaching spiritual seekers, these dedicated Christ-followers wanted to know how small groups could help them be even more effective in ministering to ex-Mormons. So Mary explained the principles that would help them design a small-group strategy that fit their vision, reflecting who they are and whom they want to reach. Together they created a "nesting vision"—a small-group vision that supported their church's vision—and dreamed God's dreams for how to use their gifts and passions to connect with the broader community.

As Mary described it, it was "goose-bump stuff." They produced all kinds of creative ideas. One dad's dream group was to meet with the fathers of the homeschooled children in the community; he wanted to mentor guys on what it means to be a loving father and a supportive husband. As he dreamed God's dreams, his own vision of God's call on his life became clearer and clearer. He laid out detail after detail of how he would create a small group to serve those around him.

A band of already-dedicated pray-ers in the church had an even sharper insight as to how foundational they were to the body's vision. They were the spiritual warriors upholding the work of those interacting with a spiritually darkened community. In a day-long training session, these excited church members created outside-the-box small groups that reflected their passions, interests, and gifts, groups created in response to the challenge, "What kind of small group would you rearrange *your* schedule for?"

By the time the training ended, Mary hated to leave this little big-visioned group. She was drawn in by the love, energy, and passion of their focused calling in the area of small groups. It was contagious—they couldn't wait to get started. Over and over they thanked her for opening their eyes to see small groups in a fresh light, for releasing them to dream God's dreams.*

Kelloggsville Church, an eight-hundred-member suburban congregation in Kentwood, Michigan, caught the vision too. The church had had small groups for some time, but they'd pretty much fizzled and failed due to exhausted leadership. The staff was already overworked, with no time to devote to a struggling small-group system; there was no one to guide the ministry or encourage and support the small-group leaders. So the staff watched as the number of small groups dwindled to just two (*two,* for eight hundred members). Meanwhile, the church was going through a time of clarifying its mission and vision, and when the leadership looked at effective ministry, they saw plainly that small groups needed to be a part of both caring for its members and reaching out to

*All the stories in this book are true. Some of the names and details have been changed to protect the privacy of individuals.

the community. Kelloggsville had reached a transition point, and major change was needed.

It was at that juncture, clearly God's timing, that Diane, a member of the church and a small-group workshop trainer who'd just become familiar with principle-based groups, shared with key staff and weary leaders the freedom and freshness of growing people through these groups (and, coincidentally, growing the groups themselves). Together they designed a strategy built on the gifts and passions of their people, a strategy in keeping with what they believed God intended for their church. By tapping into the leaders' gifts and passions, the church's entire small-group approach radically changed, and the leaders and attendees changed as well. As they were released to dream God's dreams, people created groups out of new enthusiasm. The number and kinds of groups they developed increased dramatically. They became excited about their groups, taking personal ownership because they'd helped design them. They developed a small-group nesting vision that fit their church's commitment to outreach and care.

One of the newly formed groups came out of Kelloggsville's "Sportsperson's Club," a growing side-door ministry of the church begun several years earlier. The Sportsperson's Club was the dream of Pastor Maury DeYoung, who longed to reach a group often overlooked by the church—weekend hunters and fishermen. Maury's own love of the outdoors created a natural link for reaching people who spent their weekends hunting and fishing rather than in church. Accordingly, on Thursday nights, people gathered to learn tips about deer hunting, tying flies for fly-fishing, bow-and-arrow target practice, and a host of other topics to engage outdoor enthusiasts. As he reached these avid sportspersons with the things they loved and that motivated them, he built relationships and led them to see the Creator behind the creation they enjoyed. Out of that foundation, Maury continues to facilitate small groups of men willing to explore the Bible and share their stories. What started as one group of about six people with a passion for hunting and fishing and for seeing God at work has grown to a large ministry that has touched the lives of thousands in western Michigan. Watching God work has been exciting, and new ministry avenues continue to emerge.

A couple of women in the church developed a strong desire to reach the wives of these outdoor enthusiasts. Starting small, these women created an affirming, we-care-about-*you* environment to support the wives who became "deer widows" during the fall hunting season. Women who had never before been in a church responded to the community invitation and found a welcoming place to enjoy hanging out with other women. In fact, the woman who initially appeared most uncomfortable being in a church building was the last to leave at the end of the first evening. "I haven't had this much fun in years!" she told the group leaders. "I'll come again."

New kinds of groups, new people reached. All because Kelloggsville Church was open to dreaming God's dreams for their community and open to a new way of thinking about small groups. Both these churches, in Kentwood and Salt Lake City, illustrate the importance of the foundation for experiencing God's blessing on your small-group ministry: *Be rooted in God's will.*

These leaders had a vision for what God was calling them to be and to do, and they had a vision for how small groups would facilitate that call. They were willing to let this vision be the driving force in determining what they did, and they learned the significance of tuning their hearts to listen to God before they did anything else.

Tuning our hearts to beat with God's is an essential beginning point. *That's* what marks the ministries He blesses, and we have benefited from a host of small-group pioneers who have provided excellent fodder for us, contributing mightily to our understanding of God's intent for small groups. For instance, we have learned invaluable lessons from the Alcoholics Anonymous Twelve-Step model, Paul Yonggi Cho's cell model, Carl George's meta-model, Lyman Coleman's serendipity model, and the Willow Creek challenge to become "a church *of* small groups, not *with* small groups." The Alpha course has been embraced worldwide, drawing people to Christ.

These are just a few examples of the models that have informed our understanding of small groups. Again, they have been influential because their leaders listened for God's voice and were faithful in discerning what He was up to in their ministry. Whether Full Gospel Church, Willow Creek, Saddleback, or other thriving ministries, their leaders pursued the answer to the question, "What is God doing here?" and then did it with passion and purpose. They're God-centered and people-related; this is the most important thing we learn from them, for though the models are valuable, it is *zeal for following God's call* and the *underlying principles behind the models* that are fundamental.

We can learn from what they have done, but we cannot imitate another's vision and make it our own. Bill Easum, president of Easum, Bandy and Associates (*www.easumbandy.com*), put it this way:

> *Too many leaders try to "cut and paste" someone else's vision into their setting. Copycat visions always fail. Leaders can't inspire what they have not lived and spiritually died to.*

Trying to do this leads to what Wes Roberts (in an e-mail to a bunch of Promise Keepers guys) called "Paul Yonggi Cho depression," a phenomenon that happens when people follow, to a T, all that Cho has done to build his Full Gospel Church in Seoul, South Korea, to a membership numbering in the hundreds of thousands—but without the dramatic (or any) results. Cho is successful because he's been obedient to the vision and call *he* received from God. God has blessed him because he was faithful to do what God directed *him* to do. In the wonderful diversity God has created, He's planned something unique for *your* church too. Discovering what that is and joining Him in the work will bring joy and energy to your small-group ministry.

Being God-centered and people-related means that God's will comes first. We need to focus on Him because *He* is the one with the perfect plan for our small-group ministry. Psalm 127:1 tells us that "unless the LORD builds the house, its builders labor in vain." It's *God's* work, not ours. We are His hands and feet and voice, following His guidance and listening for His voice through earnest, fervent prayer, both individually as leaders and also with others who come alongside and join the work. The band of faithful prayer warriors in the tiny Salt Lake City church knew this. Because they were in tune with God's heart, they could clearly see the vision He had for using them to reach ex-Mormons through their small-group ministry.

A God-centered vision also means diligently studying His Word to clarify the vision He gives us and then being accountable to one another in staying focused on that vision. It means we learn from what God models in His Story (the Bible). Regular reflection and evaluation will ensure that we are God-centered and people-related rather than people-centered and God-related.

We'll learn from His example: He is a relational God, reaching people where they are, not where He wants them to be. Beginning in Eden, He "walked in the Garden" to see what was growing, what needed pruning, what needed exposing. It was in His walking around the Garden in the cool of the day that He called to Adam, "Where are you?" offering Adam a place of honesty and confession. He met Adam at his point of need, just as He meets each of us at ours, just as He desires that we meet others at theirs.

We learn also from Christ's example in the Gospels. He had a mentoring relationship with a tight circle of three—Peter, James, and John. In addition, He taught and lived with twelve disciples who were totally different from one another and yet united in one purpose. Furthermore, Jesus daily interacted with people, loving them and healing them, both individually and in groups.

Once again: A God-sized small-group vision celebrates the diversity He created. It's large enough to include a wide variety of small groups. It frees people to listen to God's voice and use their God-given gifts. It's not controlling but empowering, not draining but energizing. *It's organic and fluid in nature, changing its methods according to the surrounding cultural landscape but changeless in its central purpose of growing people on their journey to becoming completely committed Christ-followers.* It acknowledges that new groups constantly form, and when their purpose has been accomplished, they end. It's a vision that presumes change, constantly asking, "What is God doing right here, right now, with this person, with this group, in this place?" It's a vision built on mutual trust and accountability. It's filled with the anticipation of God's provision and blessing.

Putting God's agenda first is also wonderfully freeing for small-group leaders. They no longer need to feel that the weight of the small-group world rests on their shoulders. They can release that burden to God, knowing He will bring to completion and bless what we do when we stay on our knees and submit to His leading. It means we're free to move to a new stage of ministry when He calls us to it, trusting Him to provide leadership for our small group or for the entire ministry, especially if we've been faithful in sharing His vision for small groups with others. It means small groups may exist for a season and a reason, but not forever—it isn't failure if they end when they've completed their God-ordained purpose. The bottom line is this: *There is incredible freedom when God comes first and we come second, when we are God-centered and people-related.*

The tiny church in Salt Lake City and the large church in Kentwood caught a God-sized vision for small groups. In designing groups based on a wide variety of gifts and passions, both churches reflect their unique culture, cultures that celebrate diversity and individuality. They also reflect their Creator, who designed this diversity and therefore delights in it. They tuned their will to His, and they're experiencing firsthand that when our will is one with God's, we'll be ready for the wild, wonderful ride of working with the people He places in our path, people with whom He wants us to share His love.

Summary Questions

The following questions (and those at the end of subsequent chapters) are designed to help you in your quest to become rooted in God's will and to discern His will for your small-group ministry.

1. What is God doing in your church? What is He already blessing that you can capitalize on?

2. What is God asking you to give up, to die to, in order to pursue the vision He's giving you?

3. What is unique about your church that God could use in a special way?

4. How can small groups help to fulfill the mission God has for you?

5. With what resources has God blessed your church?

6. What needs of your community might God be calling you to meet?

7. What gifts and passions has God given the people in your church?

CHAPTER TWO:

GROW PEOPLE, NOT PROGRAMS

A few years ago I (Betty) started a small-group Bible study for women who were employed. The group members came for a variety of reasons. Joanne came to build relationships; she was new to the community and wanted to get to know other women in her neighborhood. Linda was looking for support; her recent divorce had left her broken and unsure of herself, deeply in need of a place to heal. Connie was a spiritual seeker desiring to reconnect with the Christian roots she'd abandoned when she married a man who had no interest in the church. Diane was a mature Christian committed to reaching others while she also grew in her own walk with Jesus. The fact that we all juggled the demands of home and the workplace gave us something in common.

Jill was part of our group too, for a whole gamut of reasons. I first met her at a Little League baseball game; our sons were on the same team, and we were huddled with other loyal moms in the bleachers, cheering for our kids. With almost no prompting on my part, Jill chatted away about her life story, then turned to me and asked, "So what else would you like to know?" She was delightful! It was our Little League connection that brought us together, but it was our growing friendship that led her to say yes to my invitation to join the Bible study I was starting in my home. She also said yes because of her spiritual hunger. She was pretty mad at God, seeing Him as a rock in her life—"cold, hard, and unfeeling." In the beginning she came in hopes that He would "zap" her, as she put it, giving her a dramatic spiritual conversion experience.

She didn't make it easy for Him, challenging Him and the group on every front. He isn't fair, she insisted. What about the people in Africa? she wanted to know. What did they do to deserve such a tough life? Her questions were hard, her pursuit of answers relentless. Through it all, we grew to love her deeply, and she us. "I need you guys," she would say. "You help me get connected to God." She had deep issues in her life, felt needs that required years of our meeting together before she trusted us enough to share. It was ten years before I ever heard her pray aloud. She, more than anyone else, taught me the importance of taking great care to discern what God is doing in people's lives and then meeting them at that point of need.

Small groups are all about people because the crown of God's creation is people. It's *people* He wants us to build, not programs; He delights in the variety He created, and He wants us to delight in it too. That's why small groups play such an important part in how Christ builds His church—we share His love with people, relating to them, meeting their needs, releasing their passions, honoring their differences, and seeing them grow spiritually.

When we focus on building programs instead of growing people, we miss the living, breathing dimension of small-group ministry, which then becomes mechanistic, as though making sure all the pieces of a puzzle fit together or all the cogs in a wheel work properly. There's nothing vital and dynamic about *that*. People are not components of a machine; they think and feel and love and laugh and experience pain and loss. They are growing, organic beings, not mechanical parts. People are like plants in a greenhouse. If you leave plants alone for six months, you never know what you might find when you get back. They may be dead from lack of light or water. Or they may be overgrown with weeds. Or they may have experienced so much growth that they're bursting from their pots, needing to be transplanted in order to continue to grow.

Again, the foundation of any successful small-group ministry is God. Once we answer the question, "What is *God* up to in our church?" and understand His call for our small-group ministry, we need to ask, "What are the *people* around us up to?" We need to focus on the individuals He wants us to reach, not on the institutions we think He wants us to build. We need to see people as God sees them—dynamic, unique, created by Him and precious in His sight—not as a means by which to grow our program. Remember: Wherever people are in their spiritual journey is where God asks us to meet them.

All of us are on a pilgrimage, and very few of us are at exactly the same point of spiritual development at the same time. It's unrealistic to expect that the same kind of small group will be a good fit for everyone or even, as illustrated above, that everyone in a group will have the same spiritual needs. Thinking of these differences as myriad points on a small-group continuum helps us to gauge where people are.

SMALL-GROUP CONTINUUM:
Start Wherever People Are

Curious and Cautious ----------------➤ Completely Committed to Christ

---

Individuals move around on this continuum, depending on what's happening in their lives. People may be walking closely with Jesus when a life-changing experience rocks what they have believed to be true, and they take several giant steps backward in trusting God. It might be an unfaithful marriage partner, the onset of cancer, a job loss, or the death of a child, but whatever the situation, it makes them question God and the foundation of their trust. Some who experience these same situations are propelled forward in their faith, are drawn closer to God, and dramatically deepen their roots. Still others bounce around, one day in the valley of despair, another on a spiritual mountaintop. The journey to becoming like Christ isn't always a smooth one; this is why we must take such care to discern where people are, endeavoring to reach them at their point of need.

Nobody illustrates sensitivity to people's needs better than Jesus; consider, for example, the story of the two followers on the road to Emmaus (Luke 24). He joined them as they were walking together, talking about the earthshaking events that had recently taken place in Jerusalem—Jesus' trial and crucifixion. He, of course, was fully aware of what had happened, knowing far more about the situation than they did. But He didn't begin by proclaiming His resurrection or demonstrating His new power over the grave. Instead, He asked what they were discussing. He joined the conversation at precisely the level of understanding they had, exactly where they were on their spiritual journey. Later, over dinner, when they were ready, He opened their eyes to see Him fully: Jesus began with where they were, and over time He led them to where He wanted them to be. Starting where people already are on their path to knowing Jesus, then nudging them forward in a way that fits them, shows respect for their individuality and honors how God is working in their lives.

This brings us back to why one-size-fits-all small groups don't work well, which I (Betty) learned in a very personal way. For several years I was a stay-at-home mom who, along with other moms in my neighborhood, raised my family and attended a community-oriented Coffee Break Bible study. Together we shared our lives and our faith journeys. It united our whole neighborhood . . . but then our neighborhood changed. Two of my friends moved away. One discovered her husband was addicted to prescription drugs. Another reentered the work force and built new friends there.

My life changed too. I went through a painful divorce, with all of its accompanying grief and shame. My teenage sons moved out of state with their dad, and I needed to rejoin the work force full time in order to support myself. This wasn't the way life was supposed to be. It was precisely at that time, however, that God brought into my life people who were also experiencing that life wasn't what they'd expected.

During the early years of my single-again status, I shared my home with a number of young women in crisis pregnancies, becoming their shepherding mom at a frightening and confusing time of their lives. Most had little or no interest in God or being part of a community of believers, and somehow inviting them to my church Bible study seemed like the wrong way to try reaching them. I was at a loss as to how they could be connected to the Jesus I loved and in whom I found strength and comfort.

Nevertheless, God provided other ways, other kinds of small groups. Mimi found connection in a support group for young, single pregnant women; so did Hillary. Under the loving guidance of a Christian social worker, these broken women grew spiritually. Mimi herself eventually became a small-group leader.

At my invitation, Tina, one of the young birthmoms, actually did attend a Coffee Break study with me—only once, and probably out of a sense of obligation. Watching her fidget and squirm through the entire hour, I felt her discomfort and regretted putting my agenda above her needs. Even though I knew that what she needed most was to know Jesus, I wasn't sensitive to where she was on her journey with Him. After the meeting, I thanked her for giving it a try and promised I wouldn't pressure her again. She was relieved, and I was grateful God gave me another chance to build her trust in me, a trust I wanted to cultivate rather than violate.

I was privileged to be in the delivery room when Tina gave birth to a beautiful baby girl. I was there when she selflessly put her daughter's needs above her own desires, placing her newborn into the arms of the loving childless couple she'd selected to parent her baby. I held Tina in my arms as she cried over her loss.

When she moved out of my home, I thought she would move out of my life as well. But God had other plans. Tina stayed in touch, and I learned to simply follow the nudging of the Holy Spirit, connecting her to Jesus in ways she could handle. After four years, Tina committed her life to Christ; God softened her until she was compelled to respond. "I should have done it before," she confessed. "I was just too stubborn." She's *still* stubborn, but God is using her tenacity to shape her into a beautiful woman. He is walking the journey with her, and so am I.

My own spiritual journey—together with those who've walked alongside me—has taught me a new sensitivity to others. I was encouraged by the people who reached out to me in my brokenness and weren't afraid of my pain. They remained with me through the healing process, never asking me to be further along than I was. In my times of deepest shame and loss, they helped me see myself through the eyes of Jesus, the eyes of grace. They reflected Christ to me; I've tried to do the same with others.

Finding small-group compatibility for the people God has asked us to reach will be crucial in helping them to take the next step on their path. When we push people along the continuum before they're ready, we're putting our agenda ahead of their needs. We promote our programs at the expense of the people we serve, and in so doing we may impede the very outcome we hope to attain. Though we may meet someone at a point on his or her spiritual journey where nudging (and perhaps even calling for commitment) is appropriate, we need to do so *with clear direction from God*. Running ahead of Him often has disastrous results. We must wait for His timing.

One church learned the importance of respecting individual spiritual journeys just in time. When Promise Keepers challenged men to get into accountability groups, an enthusiastic leader took it to heart; he called me (David) looking for help on how to start accountability groups for all the men in his church. Though I appreciated his enthusiasm, I also felt I needed more information about his situation—especially the men he was targeting—before I could help him launch full-fledged accountability groups. My first question was, "How old is your church?"

"Three years old," he told me, indicating a fairly young congregation.

Then I asked, "Where are these men on their spiritual journey with Christ?"

He reflected thoughtfully a few minutes and then acknowledged that most were either seekers or very new in their faith.

Finally I inquired, "How well do these men know one another?"

There was a long pause before he answered. I think he was beginning to see where I was headed, and his voice softened. "Not very well," he admitted.

He'd never really had occasion to consider all the dynamics in his church, but now he considered them carefully. In truth, most of the guys attending were still young in their mutual relationships. So I posed this question: "How likely is it that accountability groups will succeed in a very young church with brand-new Christians who don't know each other well?"

That put things into a more realistic perspective for this eager young pastor. He could see that in his particular situation, trying to start a men's ministry by implementing full-fledged accountability groups was a setup for failure. He was putting his own desires, well-intentioned though they were, above the needs of the men in his church. His original starting point for the accountability groups was where he wanted the men to be, not where they actually were. A more non-threatening, entry-level small group seemed a safer (and more helpful) place to begin.

Generally speaking, men expose their inner thoughts *cautiously*. One of their primary concerns is, "What are you going to do with the information I give you?" Trust is foundational for seeing them open their lives to one another, and *building trust takes time*. Many of the men this leader wanted to reach were too new in the church, too new in their faith, and too new to one another to have the foundation necessary for effective accountability groups. Starting relationship-building groups, for example, would help to prepare them for accountability groups later on. The latter group can and does work, but when it does, it's because the people involved are at the point in their spiritual journey, and on the small-group continuum, where they're ready and eager for this kind of connectedness. Again, we need to start with where people are, not where we want them to be.

Six Personal Motivations

Why do people get involved in small groups? We can't answer this question without understanding the individuals. We need to "live in their skin," think like they think. We need to see what gives them joy or pain, what hurts and heartaches they carry, what makes them laugh or cry, what ignites their passions and touches their souls. We need to understand the factors that influence their choices.

Jesus knew how to do this. When His friends Mary and Martha grieved the death of their brother, Lazarus, Jesus wept, even though He knew he would raise Lazarus from the dead (John 11). He felt the pain of His friends.

When He showed up at the well in Samaria (John 4), He was aware that the woman who would join Him there at midday was an outsider when it came to relationships with other women in town. She didn't draw water at the same time they did. She came alone in the heat of the day. She was avoiding people. She was different. She didn't fit. But Jesus reached out to her right where she was, talked with her when others wouldn't, giving her a place to belong when no one else did. And because He met her exactly where she was, appealing to the void in her life, she was open to His message. She couldn't wait to share the news: Come and meet a man who "told me everything I ever did"—*and still wants a relationship with me*. Relationship-building motivates people.

When Jesus spotted Zacchaeus perched in a sycamore tree (Luke 19), He knew the man was looking to be embraced. As a tax collector for the hated Roman government, Zacchaeus didn't find much acceptance from his fellow Jews; the fact that he used his position to cheat them isolated him even further. And he was short—short enough so that people noticed—another reason to feel rejected. Something inside, some deeply felt need, motivated him to climb a tree to see Jesus. Jesus responded by giving him exactly what he needed: acceptance and affirmation. He could have singled out anyone, but He chose Zacchaeus: "Come down. . . . I must stay at your house today." The Lord's simple act of responding to Zacchaeus's need softened his hardened heart and made him a passionate Christ-follower.

The ten men Jesus healed (Luke 17) were together because they had something in common: leprosy. Jesus healed all of them, though only one in the group returned to thank Him. He saw their need, and He responded to it.

Jesus also honored the passion—and faith—of the four men who lowered their paralyzed friend through a roof to place him in front of Jesus (Mark 2). They believed in His power to heal, and He rewarded their faith. Jesus didn't even ask the paralyzed man to have faith; His friends' faith was enough.

Jesus recognized spiritual hunger in a person. When Nicodemus was hesitant to meet with Jesus in broad daylight, Jesus met him at night (John 3). Patiently Jesus answered his questions, neither mentioning the clandestine nature of their encounter nor ridiculing the man's meager faith. When Nicodemus came, his head was filled with academic questions; when he left, his heart was connected to Christ. Jesus met him where he was, and Nicodemus had the freedom to respond in a way he understood.

We learn from Jesus' example. We learn to tune in to the people in our lives and to the culture in which they live. We live in a complex, fast-paced society that makes innumerable demands on people's time. Many don't have the time to get involved in a small group, but many do. Why?

The competition for participation in a small group is *every other possible use of time*. Why, when there are so many schedule options, would a person intentionally carve out time to be involved in a small group? That's what we need to find out. The ultimate question we want people to answer is, *What kind of small group would you rearrange your schedule to be a part of?* The answers vary, but the common themes revolve around these six motivations:

(1) *relationship-building;*
(2) *felt needs;*
(3) *affinity;*
(4) *passions;*
(5) *spiritual hunger; and*
(6) *service-oriented tasks.*

When we tap into what motivates people and then meet that need, they're likely to be receptive to taking a closer look at Jesus.

RELATIONSHIP-BUILDING

In our small groups, we'll meet people like the Samaritan woman. We need to recognize what motivates them and then help them build relationships and find a place to belong. When Maggie first joined a Bible study, she had no intention of getting to know God or His Word; she was trying to nab a husband! The man she had in her sights was a Christian, a member of the church where a women's Coffee Break Bible study was held. She wanted to build relationships with the women in this church so the guy she had her eye on would take her seriously and be open to a committed relationship with her.

She was warmly welcomed by the women in her small group—accepted right where she was—and built wonderful friendships with them, exactly what she'd hoped to accomplish. But she also gained something she'd never even considered: she fell deeply in love with Jesus. And eventually, after she committed her life to Him, she married the man of her dreams as well. She related her experience at a training workshop for future Coffee Break leaders: "I joined Coffee Break for all the wrong reasons, but God used what motivated me to draw me to Him."

A large church in Minneapolis was finding it difficult to get a group of professional women—corporate executives, medical professionals, and business owners—involved in small groups; that is, until the small-groups director talked to a few of them individually and perceived a common theme. They were disconnected from other women whose lives were like theirs; they longed to build relationships with other professional women. These women were only peripherally involved in the church at the time, but when the small-groups pastor offered them what they were seeking—connection with other women like themselves—they responded. They were leery of big agendas; they just wanted to hang out, to rub elbows with women who walked in their shoes, who understood the pressures of corporate life and juggling multiple pressures and responsibilities at home and at work.

After a period of time, however, they moved beyond the need to simply build relationships and *did* develop an agenda, one they chose together: how to share their faith in the workplace. They moved from sharing their life stories with one another to motivating one another to take their faith stories to work. This would never have worked as a starting place, but because the church's leadership began with where they were on their faith journey and responded to their need, they were given the freedom to grow into deeper fellowship and spiritual challenge.

FELT NEEDS

Responding to people's felt needs often opens them to small groups in a way that touches their lives. With men, this isn't always easy—they tend to be somewhat resistant, like Stuart. A well-known cardiac surgeon in a major metropolitan area, Stuart was an independent kind of guy. Though his wife was a believer, he was a spiritual skeptic who thought all Christians had their heads in the sand. Even so, quality parenting was important to him. When his wife told him about a small group in their church that focused on how to be a good dad, he signed up.

He signed up because it struck a chord in his life. He wasn't ready to invest in his own spiritual growth, but he wanted to know what it took to have a good relationship with his kids. In that group of dads, through game plans and chalk-talks and interacting with a bunch of guys who had the same desire, Stuart not only learned about being a father, he learned about his heavenly Father as well. Two years after he joined that small group, he attended a Promise Keepers event with some guys from his church. He leaned over to his small-group leader and said, "You know what? Two years ago you wouldn't have caught me dead here." He responded to a felt need, which eventually opened the door to learn about God as well.

Just one short year after that Promise Keepers event, Stuart held hands with four nurses at the bedside of a church staff member facing an emergency appendectomy . . . and prayed for her. From profound skepticism to leading in prayers of faith—and it all came out of Stuart's desire to be a good dad.

AFFINITY

People are also open to getting involved in small groups when they have a strong affinity with other group members. Affinity groups are common entry points; one church, desiring to build bridges to its community, offered a small group for knitters and quilters. A non-threatening place for people to build relationships and share a common interest ended up being one of the most enjoyable small groups in the church. The women couldn't wait to get together every week. They built deep friendships with one another, exchanging much more than quilting patterns. They shared not only the gift of their handiwork but also the gift of themselves.

Many life-stage groups are affinity groups: Parents-of-preschoolers groups, empty-nester groups, and parenting-your-parents groups all share an affinity. We can create openness to spiritual growth simply by accepting and nurturing people through the transitions of their lives— by meeting them where they are, rather than where we want them to be.

PASSIONS

Another motivator for getting involved in a group is that of connecting with people's passions. Tammi was passionate about the environment, but she wasn't too sure about Jesus. She was new to our (David's) church and obviously a seeker, but, as she put it, "If your God doesn't care about the environment, then I don't care about your God." That was a challenge for me; I gave her a book on the environment by a Christian author that I thought might challenge her presuppositions about God's perspective. It stretched her thinking and helped her to see that God really does care about the environment because He made it and loves it, that stewardship of the earth is very much a Christian theme. By connecting with Tammi's passion, I helped to create a space in which she could accept the invitation to be part of a small group. By seeing that her passion was God's passion too, she began the journey in a small group to major life transformation.

SPIRITUAL HUNGER

Sometimes people are at the point on their faith journey where they can no longer ignore God knocking on the door of their heart. They *know* something is missing in their lives and they're ready to confront it. Jeff was one such person; he was not a Christian but had a spiritual hunger. He approached me (David) and told me that he'd really like to have a Bible study downtown with a bunch of male colleagues.

Wow! I already had visions of leading multiple groups of non-Christians (just like Jeff) in Bible studies, impacting all of downtown Minneapolis. What an opening! So I asked him whom he had in mind to invite. All the guys he named were men he worked with and admired. They were all committed Christians! So much for my plan.

Even though this wasn't exactly what I had in mind, I was at least wise enough to ask Jeff to tell me more and to let him lead the way. He'd been watching these men and noticed that they had something in their lives he didn't have, something he wanted. What Jeff envisioned wasn't at all what I thought it would be, but I listened to where he was and encouraged him to invite his co-workers to join him in a workplace Bible study. You can imagine their surprise—and delight—in joining their friend's journey to know Jesus. Jeff's spiritual hunger started it all, and those downtown guys had the joy and privilege of watching Jeff commit his life to Christ and grow in his faith.

When people start asking questions about the Christian faith, even in a challenging way, it may be that God is moving their hearts and stirring a deep spiritual hunger to which they'll be compelled to respond. Our sensitivity to their need creates an opportunity to connect them with a small group to meet that need. Sandy almost missed her neighbor Leesha's openness to the Holy Spirit. Leesha seemed to have it all together, and there was no room for God in her life. She accepted Sandy's invitation to attend a Bible study group and seemed to enjoy interacting with the people there, but as far as Sandy could see, Leesha didn't need Jesus. She had all the arguments against Christianity neatly rehearsed and ready to recite whenever Sandy tried to nudge open the door to her heart.

Sandy came to a workshop I (Betty) led at her church on how to lead someone to Christ. At one point, after sharing a gospel presentation with the group, I asked for a volunteer to role-play a non-Christian to whom I would present the gospel, putting into practice what they had just learned. Sandy volunteered to role-play, taking on Leesha's personality and objections, as if it were Leesha there instead of Sandy. She put me through the mill, objecting here, challenging there, and in the end she told me she needed to think about it, that she wasn't ready to commit her life to Christ. It wasn't the sort of role-playing I'd envisioned for the group . . . but for Sandy, it felt very true to her experience with Leesha.

A friend of Sandy's, who was also attending the workshop, challenged her. "You're presuming to know how Leesha will respond," she gently told her. "Why don't you let her answer for herself?" A few weeks later, Sandy did exactly as her friend suggested. She presented the gospel to Leesha, just as I'd done in the workshop. To Sandy's astonishment, Leesha invited Christ into her heart and committed her life to Him. Everything she'd been learning in her small-group Bible study had begun to make sense. God had softened her heart, and she was ready to make Him the Lord of her life.

We must never underestimate the power of God in someone's life. When we're rooted in His will and open to His leading (both in us and in the lives of others), He may use us to show someone how to satisfy their spiritual hunger simply by our responding to where they're at on their spiritual journey.

SERVICE-ORIENTED TASKS

When Bob was challenged with "What kind of small group would you rearrange your schedule to be a part of?" at a People Together training workshop, he knew exactly how to respond. He loved working with his hands, and he loved helping others. He put those two together and started a small group called Bob's Builders. He couldn't wait to get started, and he didn't! The day after the workshop he got on the phone and invited a bunch of guys to join him in doing odd jobs and repair work for needy people in their church and community—mostly single moms and the elderly. They even painted the church nursery!

Best of all, this service-oriented group connected men who wouldn't have been open to another kind of group. Jack was one of those guys. His wife, Maria, had begged him to get involved, but Jack was leery of those "touchy-feely groups," as he called them. Then he heard about Bob's Builders, and he was one of the first to sign up. Maria was amazed. Week after week he faithfully attended, painting houses, repairing porches, roofing, and doing any number of odd jobs.

After a while Maria noticed that Jack was talking less and less about the work he was doing and more and more about the guys he was working with. This was more than just a work group: It was a place of genuine friendship. Bob's Builders began to care deeply for one another. By tapping into what motivated guys like himself, guys who wanted to help others in a practical way, Bob opened the door for them to grow in their relationships and their faith as well.

Small-Group Definition

A principle-based small-group system that celebrates the diversity God created and embraces a variety of groups requires a broad definition of "small group." The working definition we use is this:

> *A small group is an intentional face-to-face gathering, varying in size and meeting regularly together to accomplish an agreed-upon Christian purpose.*

A small group isn't just any old group of people thrown together. Small groups are intentional, existing for a specific purpose that every member understands and embraces. As mentioned, the size may vary.

Accountability groups, due to the highly confidential nature of such a gathering, may be as small as three. Short-term working groups may number in the twenties or thirties. We don't want to arbitrarily limit how God works.

"Meeting regularly" will also mean different things for different groups. For several years a few professional women in ministry developed a virtual small group that provided encouragement and emotional and prayer support for one another via e-mail as well as through occasional phone calls. They shared both their personal lives and their professional lives, creating an opportunity to develop deep and spiritually rich relationships. Uniquely, the "meeting regularly" was at an intense annual weekend retreat where they shut out the world and laughed together, cried together, learned together, and prayed together. This was the only face-to-face time when all of them were present. Until several members moved away and they disbanded, that yearly weekend retreat was a priority for all of them.

Gordon, a pastor with a heart for reaching spiritual seekers, also happens to be a scratch golfer. He started a "gospel and golf" small group, a foursome that meets for five hours—the approximate time it takes them to play eighteen holes and spend some time talking together. Gordon shares his expertise about golf with the guys, and they share their objections to and questions about Christianity with him. In the north country, where Gordon lives, it is by necessity a seasonal group; however, the bond built by those involved testifies to how God is using this leader's godly love and athletic ability to reach men who might more readily spend their Sundays on the links than in church.

An open-ended definition of a small group provides room for God's surprises. It frees both those who lead groups and those who support leaders to welcome diversity. It challenges everyone to focus on God's vision for small groups in individual churches.

When we listen to God's voice and grow people instead of programs, we never know how He'll work in people's lives. All He asks of us is that we stay close enough to hear Him speaking to us. He may work through people's passions, such as Tammi's interest in the environment. A Christian book, on her pastor's recommendation, began to soften Tammi's heart on her journey to knowing Jesus as Savior and Lord. After she committed her life to Christ, she went on to lead a small group for others who were interested in environmental issues.

Stuart responded to the appeal to be a better dad. Jeff simply wanted to be in a Bible study with men he longed to emulate. Maggie wanted a husband. Jill needed acceptance. A group of gifted quilters found community by sharing a common interest. Each of these people was motivated by something different; each was at a different place on his or her spiritual journey.

In addition, motivations change along the journey. What compelled Stuart to get involved in a small group initially became secondary when he met his heavenly Father. Jill's motivations were a hodgepodge of several things, and she might have responded on several levels. Nothing is cut-and-dried when it comes to dealing with people. It's both frustrating and exhilarating.

But we *can* be assured of this: When we put God's agenda first and walk through the doors He opens, we will meet people at a variety of points along the way. From the curious and cautious seeker to the completely committed Christ-follower, God wants us to help people grow. And He wants us to do it in a way that acknowledges and celebrates the delightful diversity He created.

Summary Questions

1. Has your church been building people or programs? What indicators verify your answer?

2. What do you see as the biggest challenges to implementing a principle-based small-groups ministry?

3. What changes might you need to make to become more people-related?

4. In what ways are you meeting people where they are, as opposed to where you want them to be?

5. Who might join you in helping to create a people-related strategy for small groups?

CHAPTER THREE:

CREATE ATMOSPHERES FOR A DIVERSE SET OF PEOPLE

Ruth hurried to answer the phone's demanding ring. The older woman calling gave her name and then paused. "You probably don't remember me," she apologized, "but I was at the small-groups workshop you led yesterday. You asked us to think about what kind of group we might want to lead. I wasn't sure my idea was a good one, so I didn't say anything. But I've been wondering about it. I'd like to share it with you and see what you think."

This was a first for Ruth—she'd never had someone call the day *after* a workshop to complete an assignment she'd given the day before. It made her curious. "There really are no right or wrong answers," she assured. "Please, by all means, tell me what kind of group you're thinking about." Then she listened as the woman shared what was dear to her heart. Her idea was to start a small group that would commit to visiting the shut-ins in their church and small-town community. Afterward the group would get together and pray for each of the people they'd visited. Her earnest compassion was contagious. It was obvious she'd done some serious thinking and praying about the idea; now she needed the affirmation that it was an important group to start.

"Do you think it would work?" she asked. Ruth could hardly contain her delight. "Of course!" she exclaimed. "What a creative idea, and what a wonderful need it would fill!" Ruth marveled at the creativity God gives His people, the diverse ways He uses their passions to touch the lives of others. This was one kind of group, she freely admitted, that she never would have thought to implement. After chatting a few minutes more, the two ended the conversation. The woman was greatly encouraged and motivated to begin, and Ruth promised to be supportive in any way she could.

A few hundred miles away, Sam, a small-group trainer like Ruth, was talking to Karen, a Coffee Break leader who was also concerned with touching the lives of older women. While Coffee Break is directed toward women who have never before studied the Bible or who aren't joined to a church community, the women in Karen's small group were quite different. They were in their sixties and seventies, women who had been a part of the church for years and years. Attending church was part of the culture in which they'd been raised; they couldn't imagine anything different. Theirs was a quiet, private faith, not something they shared easily with others. They hardly seemed like an outreach audience, but Karen was wise enough to see God's hand in leading them to come to the group. She believed He had a special plan for their being there, and that He'd called her to be part of it. She cared deeply for them.

"We're not really a Coffee Break," Karen confessed, almost apologetically, "at least not the way the other groups are." Sam saw it differently and was quick to reassure Karen. She applauded her sensitivity to God's leading and her willingness to accept these older women just as they were. It had been a bold step for them to even join the group; Coffee Break's discussion format was markedly different from the teaching format they were used to. Having Karen guide them with questions, while encouraging them to discover biblical truths for themselves, was a stretching experience for them. They were quiet at first, hesitant and unsure of themselves. But Karen created an atmosphere of openness and warmth. She gently coaxed them to share their insights and their lives with one another. She comforted them when they revealed their loneliness. She listened to their fears about whether they were truly saved, their insecurities about their identity and their worth. As she led them to discover the promises of God and watched their faith blossom, she grew to love them; they grew to love her and one another as well. They laughed together and cried together and learned together, and after a while they even dared to pray out loud together.

Like the woman who envisioned caring for shut-ins, Karen's specific small-group niche was older women, a group easily overlooked when thinking about outreach in the church. Ruth and Sam rejoiced to hear their stories, grateful for all the ways God gifts His people to reach others and grow them in their faith. They were thankful that these compassionate women knew exactly how to create the right atmosphere to encourage the faith-walk of the people they nurtured. These were small groups born of passion and calling, focused on meeting the important needs of these unique people who are sometimes neglected in small-group ministries.

When we stop to think about it, it seems obvious that different people will positively respond to different kinds of small groups. We have different interests and needs, we thrive in different kinds of atmospheres, and we're at different points in our spiritual journeys. How on earth could we all ever be in the same kind of group? Obviously we can't, which is why creating different kinds of groups makes sense. In order to effectively grow people through small groups, *we need to create atmospheres for a diverse set of people.*

When Jesus said, "I will build my church," He wasn't talking about a building or an institution—He was talking about people. Among His final words to the apostles were, "Go and make disciples." The charge of Christ's church is to grow people, not programs or ministries.

There are fundamental differences between building something and growing something. When we *build* something, such as a house, we generally start with inanimate (dead) objects—lumber, nails, screws, bricks, paint, etc. We can manipulate the materials in any way we wish; we decide what we're going to do, when and how we're going to do it; we develop the plan and control the outcomes. Other than following architectural principles, we don't have to tune in to where the house is or how the house is feeling or changing during the construction process. We can choose at any time to add a patio or remodel the kitchen or wallpaper a bedroom. *Our* point of view is what matters most. Building is based on *our* decisions, the blueprints we've approved, the money and resources we have for the project.

When we *grow* something, we start with vital (living) objects. We need to be concerned with the living organism we're nurturing, not our own choices, needs, and desires. We serve what we're trying to grow rather than (as in building) having the materials serve our whims.

My (David's) early background was in botany, and after graduating from college I worked in a greenhouse nursery. We grew a wide variety of plants in about an acre and a half of greenhouses, one of which was tropical, containing plants that thrive in a rain forest. Its conditions were specifically set to grow tropical plants; the temperature was between 90 and 100 muggy degrees, giving the air the texture of a steam bath. We also had a cactus greenhouse that was notably different—its air, though also hot, was very dry, and the cacti thrived in it. In addition, we had a main greenhouse where we grew all kinds of geraniums, marigolds, fuchsia, petunias, and other perennials, adjusting the light, moisture, nutrients, and temperature for their maximum health. In yet another greenhouse we germinated plants in general. *All* the greenhouses had different atmospheres: They were all growing plants of various kinds, but each had a specific sub-climate designed so that the plants in it would mature and thrive.

The cacti would never have grown in the tropical greenhouse, the geraniums would have wilted in the arid greenhouse, and so on. The saying "a weed is just a plant out of place" was never more true! We needed to be certain that every plant was placed in its optimal atmosphere.

What all greenhouses had in common was the nurseryman. (That would be me.) It was my job every morning to walk through and ascertain the condition of the various plants, observing them closely. Was anything attacking them? Was something preventing them from getting larger? Were they getting enough moisture, the right amount of sunlight? Were they diseased? How much carbon dioxide were they receiving? I couldn't simply decide on my own to change the greenhouse conditions or to grow anything at any time I chose. I needed to determine the atmosphere around the plants, to note their stage of growth. This process was nothing like building a deck on my home.

Those of us in church leadership today, whether paid staff or volunteers, can learn lessons from the greenhouse. We need to remember that we are called to make disciples, not build structures. It's easy for us to be lured into the bigger-is-better mentality and become so busy building ministries that we forget our primary purpose is to grow people in their faith. We forget to "walk around the greenhouse," examining the conditions and seeking to adjust the atmosphere for optimal growth. This is vitally important in order for small-group members—and the ministry— to thrive.

There are two kinds of atmospheres to consider in forming small groups. One is a more general external atmosphere (reflecting the culture we're part of); the other is a personal internal atmosphere. Each is significant in understanding how both small groups and the individuals in them grow best.

General Atmosphere

Our North American cultural landscape is changing. The *general* atmosphere in which small groups once thrived is no longer the same. In prior decades of the small-group movement, models dominated, and the creators and leaders of the models largely determined what happened and how. Even within a small-group setting, there was a hierarchy of sorts. Today's culture is less receptive to top-down leadership; we must consider four notable shifts that have influenced the general atmosphere for starting small groups.

The *first* general-atmosphere change is that principles work better than models. Models have substantially informed what we know about small groups, but the principles we derive from those models are what make them endure. Models are prescriptive; principles are descriptive. Models have greater rigidity and seek to replicate themselves more or less precisely. Principles are fluid, and although they set parameters, they also allow freedom for different expressions of them. And let's face it: People are more different than they are alike! Small groups are about people, people who change and act unpredictably and laugh and cry and sometimes drive us crazy! They're not building blocks we can put together in a foreseeable way. The most effective small groups are formed around principles, not structures; small groups are as dynamic as the people in them. A life-changing small-group ministry has an underlying set of central principles that is foundational for how God transforms people.

Imitating models from secondary sources, without careful understanding of the underlying principles, rarely works. But following the principles involved in setting up small groups honors the process by which people become completely committed Christ-followers. The specific principles we have identified are:

(1) *the principle of belonging*
(2) *the principle of support*
(3) *the principle of learning retention*
(4) *the principle of life transformation*
(5) *the principle of accountability*
(6) *the principle of experimentation*
(7) *the principle of risk-taking*
(8) *the principle of synergy*
(9) *the principles of decision-making and problem-solving*

All of these things happen better when a person is in a small group than when he or she is alone. The principles build on one another, they apply both to individuals and to the life cycle of a group, and they are transferable to any kind of small group. We'll talk about them more fully in chapter 5.

A *second* general-atmosphere change is that a diverse culture desires diversity in small groups. Simply put, people want choices. Our society is no longer made up of people trying to look the same; we're more salad bowl than melting pot. We take pride in our distinctives and want them to be acknowledged, so today's small-group ministries need to be multifaceted. Not everyone has the same needs at the same time; again, an assortment of small-group choices will accommodate differing spiritual stages, differing individual needs, and a variety of cultural and personal situations. When people aren't given options, they often become restless, disappointed by unmet expectations and soon move on to something else. When we don't respect uniqueness—unrealistically expecting everyone to be on the same page—people may become disillusioned with the church, sometimes leaving it altogether.

This is what Jon and Joyce found out. As a husband/wife church-planting team, they both believed in the importance of small groups, but they faced some differences. Jon wanted to plant their new church using a cell model, where all the small groups were structured the same way. That was how they started, and, in fact, it was a good way to begin. Several months into the development of their small-group ministry, however, Joyce became familiar with the principle-based approach that provides for all kinds of small groups, and she began to rethink the one-size-fits-all mentality.

Joyce became convinced of the need to provide a variety of small groups, so she set out to persuade Jon as well. He wasn't convinced, which resulted in lively discussions that debated the pros and cons of each approach. Then a funny thing happened. Their groups that had all started the same way began to change. One wanted to be a family-oriented group that included children as an important part of their meeting time. Another wanted to focus on deeper spiritual disciplines. Another wanted to be a welcoming place for non-Christians. Though they had all begun at the same place, they didn't all end up in the same place. As Jon watched the process unfold and learned more and more about the freedom that comes from dreaming God's dreams for small groups, he became convinced it was the right direction. Principle-based groups provided the diversity that could accommodate the differences in their members. Today Jon is sold on the concept and encourages other church planters to develop it, using the gifts and passions of their small-group leaders.

That leads us to the *third* general-atmosphere change: Leaders need the freedom to design their own groups. Specific small-group leaders will carry the vision; when their gifts and passions are released and they are free to follow God's leading, they will develop groups that likewise instill passion in others. One person's passions are not enflamed by the imposition of another person's ideas—people own what they help create.

A thousand-member church in Abbotsford, British Columbia, tried it both ways. They started some small groups using a specified format and assigned study material. They began other small groups by allowing the leaders to be creative and utilize variety. There was no comparison as to which strategy worked better. The small-groups coordinator admitted:

> It's much harder to keep the groups motivated when the leaders are taking their cues from me. But the groups whose leaders were allowed to develop groups they feel passionate about are thriving. They are self-motivated. They need very little from me.

People want to give input into the small-group strategy for their church.

I (David) learned this lesson the hard way. Using Lilly grant funding, I assisted ten struggling Lutheran churches in the hope that setting up a cell-based small-group ministry would help their traditional organization grow and become spiritually vibrant. The exact opposite happened. In church after church, the small groups struggled. Some even died completely—*not* the sort of results I'd hoped for! It was a humbling experience.

Finally, in an effort to determine what was truly going on, I sat down with the churches' small-group leaders, asked questions, and listened. I found out what their vision was, what their community needed, and what the passions of their hearts were. Then I helped them start over. Instead of beginning with what *I* thought they needed, I listened to what *God* was telling them. I helped each church develop a small-group plan that fit His call for their people and their community. I learned a lot, and in the end, I was able to distill the underlying principles for growing people in small groups, principles that respect the diversity God has created in His body and allow churches to create groups reflecting that diversity.

For me (Betty), a poignant visual illustration of the "people own what they help create" idea came from Gary MacIntosh in a training session he led on team-building at a Leadership Network-sponsored event. As I sat in his workshop, Gary took out two Ritz crackers, one in each hand. One he held intact; the other he put into his mouth and chewed it up. Then he spit out the mushy cracker into his hand. He went from table to table extending both hands—one with the whole cracker and the other with the chewed up one. "Which would you rather have?" he asked.

Of course the answer was obvious.

Then he challenged us: "Do not digest everything you hear today about teams and then spit it out for your churches. They will reject it like you are rejecting this chewed-up Ritz in my hand." People need to chew on new ideas and challenges for themselves; they will own what they help create.

Admittedly, if you're the person in charge of managing the small groups in your church, this whole concept can sound a little scary. It feels much safer and more like you're in control when *you* set the structure and all the decision-making goes through *you*. Honoring how God works through His people will require letting go of power and control and trusting the Holy Spirit to guide those who are called to dream and assist.

The *fourth* general-atmosphere change explains how to do this: Create a win/win system based on spiritual accountability instead of positional authority and control. Long-term small-group effectiveness largely depends upon a supportive, accountable relationship between the leader and someone on the management team. The "control" in a principle-based system is the leader's and the manager/coach's mutual submission to the nesting vision they support. It's not an anything-goes, loosey-goosey arrangement. *All small groups need to fit within the small-group vision, a vision that begins with God's will and grows people in their relationship with Him.* That means a tap-dancing group meant to be an outreach into the community might fit, but a group intended to explore the occult through voodoo, séance, and Ouija boards definitely would not!

A win/win accountability for a leader and manager/coach is built on their love, respect, and support of each other. They thrive in mutual spiritual accountability and in their submission to the nesting vision of their small-group ministry, which is to grow people on their faith journey to know Christ. It is not based on reporting forms, rules, and control. The manager/coach's desire is to empower and free the leader to pursue God's vision for small groups. He or she does this by providing resources, praying for the leader, and doing what's necessary to help the leader succeed and become more effective. By being a listening ear and sympathetic supporter, the manager/coach will increase the leader's joy of serving. And the manager/coach will find it immensely rewarding to nurture the leaders and to see both them and their small groups not only grow but thrive.

Personal Atmosphere

The second kind of atmosphere to consider in creating growth environments for a diverse set of people is *personal*. It involves discerning what's happening in the life of each person in each group—including the leader. We encourage you, at this point, to take a piece of paper and write down your own answers to the following questions that affect an individual's "personal atmosphere":

(1) *What season of life are you in?*
(2) *What are the hurts in your life?*
(3) *Where are you on your faith journey?*
(4) *What are your passions and gifts?*
(5) *What's going on in the environment around you?*

If you were able to take the time to answer these five questions, look at your responses carefully and consider: If we were going to create a small-group atmosphere in which you would thrive, how important would it be for us to have your feedback? Very important, probably. Like the nurseryman sensitive to what's happening with the plants in his greenhouse, small-group leaders need to be aware of what's happening in the lives of their people. What's causing them pain and anxiety? What's making them question or celebrate their faith? What factors beyond their control are dragging them down? What turns them on and spurs them to action? This is critical knowledge for the work of growing people in their walk with Christ.

Ignoring the answers to these questions doesn't work; it only leads to frustrated group members and usually frustrated leaders as well. When I (Betty) was newly divorced I had a huge void in my life. I missed hanging out with couples and yearned for a place to belong. In deep spiritual hunger, I craved community with other Christians—so filled with high hopes, I joined a small-group Bible study that included five couples and me.

It didn't take long for me to experience a great deal of frustration. Our leader, a great guy, had been trained in a very specific model, and early on it became clear that the book we were studying (rather than the people in the group) was the focus of our attention. Getting through the lesson was our main goal, and we never had time to move beyond a superficial level. It's not that we didn't get along (we did), but something was missing—at least for me. We stumbled through week after week, and I kept wondering: *Is this my issue, or do others feel the same?* I needed to find out. If everyone else was content, I'd simply leave the group and look elsewhere.

We always ended our meeting with a social time. About four weeks into our study, our leader left early; the rest of us lingered over coffee and dessert. I took a deep breath and plunged in: "Do you mind letting me know why you joined this small group?" I asked one of the members. "I'm wondering what you hope to get out of our small group," I asked another.

One by one people shared their hearts. They were looking for a place of community, for a place to grow spiritually, for a place to be supported in the frustrations of parenting toddlers and rebellious teenagers. They were looking for honesty and authenticity. It became apparent that for each of us the material we were studying was really only a catalyst for bringing us together. What we all desired, even though we were at different places in our journey, was to share our lives together. We all saw it.

We didn't experience any amazing group turnaround as a result of our conversation, but it was a beginning. We worked harder at being honest with one another. We became more transparent. We struggled together until the study was over, and then we disbanded. But we learned something through the process: We *still* share a special bond when we see one another. And I became convinced anew that understanding the diversity of people's needs and what impacts who they are isn't an option; it's vital for growth.

What Season of Life Are You In?

Seasons of life encompass a variety of factors. One is based on life *age;* another is based on life *stage.* What is seasonal in your life right now? Some of us are in the career-choice season, fresh out of school and ready to plunge into work and maybe even marriage. Others are a little further down the road, wrestling with mortgages, rearing young children, and upholding all the responsibilities that come with managing a household. Maybe you're in the parenting-teenagers-and-needing-patience season. Or perhaps you're in the empty-nest season, missing the laughter and liveliness of having kids at home. There's a retirement season and a parenting-your-parents season. In addition to age-related seasons, stage-related seasons include the learning-a-new-job season, the moving-to-a-new-city season, and many, many more.

Sometimes our season of life combines age *and* stage of life. When Frank and Joan relocated to Chicago because of a job transfer, they moved away from their adult children and the city where they'd grown up, gone to college, and raised their family. It was a huge adjustment for both of them. Joan especially missed the close friendships left behind, and she sank into mild depression. Who was she without her family? Could she still make friends? How could she cope with all the losses? Frank seemed too immersed in the challenge of a new job to have time for her. Joan floundered until Molly, a small-group leader in the church they'd begun attending, invited her to attend a group called *Transitions*. "We're pretty new to Chicago too," she confessed to Joan, "and moving was a major adjustment for me. I really want to help people going through what I went through."

Joan gratefully accepted Molly's invitation. She shared her losses with people who understood because they'd experienced them too. She made new friends and became acclimated to the city, learning the best travel routes, becoming familiar with places to eat and shop, and even handling the jargon unique to her area. It was the atmosphere she needed to thrive during this season of life change; small-group leaders need to understand the life seasons of their members in order to adapt to their needs.

WHAT ARE THE WOUNDS IN YOUR LIFE?

Just as we're influenced by life seasons, so are we also impacted by painful life experiences. Where do you hurt? What are you stressed about? What concerns or problems do you face? We need to address people's woundedness and give them a place (and time) to heal before we can expect them to grow.

I (David) saw a wonderful illustration of this in a grief support group held in our church and led by my wife, Janet. Janet has exceptional gifts of mercy and encouragement. She loves people and it shows; they're drawn to her caring heart. She has a discerning spirit, knowing how to reach out to those who've lost a loved one. Under her leadership, this group, attended by both members of our church and other people from the community, became a safe place for people to mourn their losses and move forward. She patiently came alongside them as they reoriented their lives.

At some point many of the attendees faced the issue of learning to forgive. At about week six or seven, Janet invited me to come and share some thoughts on the topic of forgiveness, which I did. After I finished, two women from the group came up to talk to me. "You're the new-members pastor for this church, aren't you?" they asked. I acknowledged that, yes, I was, and they said, "We would really like to join the church."

Though I hadn't expected them to say this, I was delighted and probed a little further, asking them what led to their decision. Their response was a wonderful tribute to my wife and her ability to create an atmosphere that was sensitive to their needs, but it was especially a testimony to the life-transforming power of the Holy Spirit: "In this small group," they said, "the support and the love we received was more than we have ever experienced, and we would really like to know where it came from and what the source is."

These grief-support-group members exemplify what can happen when we tune in to people's needs. By being in an environment that dealt directly with their needs, they got spiritually unstuck and took a step toward Christ and His body. God uses many means to draw people to himself, one of which is our modeling of His love and acceptance, our awareness of where they hurt.

WHERE ARE YOU ON YOUR FAITH JOURNEY?

The answer to this question for the people in the grief group (above) was that they were consumed by the pain in their lives. We can create atmospheres that foster spiritual growth by being aware not only of people's pain and season of life, but also their season of faith. What about you? Have you been a believer for a long time? Are you not only maturing but excited about Christ? Or are you questioning your faith in God, maybe going through a dry desert experience where He seems distant? Have you been wounded by the church and become bitter and disillusioned with Christianity? Or are you just now beginning your faith journey, checking out the idea of believing in Jesus? What is your season of faith?

When Bud was in the "checking it out" season, he said to me, "Dave, I feel like I'm standing on this side of the river, and God is standing on the other side. I need something to bridge the gap to get me over there." What an opportunity to respond! I asked him, "If we can create a group that specifically speaks to bridging the gap between you and God, would you want to be a part of it?" He responded immediately, "In a minute!" We ended up creating a season-of-faith group that was called exactly that: "Bridging the Gap Between Us and God." It turned out that not only Bud but many other people were concerned about being separated from God; they likewise joined the group in order to find out about and connect with their Creator.

Lauren's season of faith related to being bored with the roles she was playing in the church. Her faith was intellectual only; she was using her administrative gifts in the structure of the church, but she wanted her faith to make a difference in a practical way. Specifically, she needed an atmosphere where she was challenged to live out her faith daily, and she found it in a small group of other women concerned about integrating their faith into their workday world. As they exhorted one another and grew in their belief, they also grew in their love for one another. In the right environment for growth, Lauren's faith moved from her head to her heart.

WHAT ARE YOUR PASSIONS AND GIFTS?

If you had to point to your cutting edge of growth, what would it be? What do you feel so strongly about that you can't deny the urge to share it with others? What are you learning? Where are you risking or experimenting in ways that expand your life? Where are you growing? These are important challenges for both leaders and group members in creating diverse atmospheres for spiritual growth.

Steve's cutting edge of growth led him to leave the company where he'd worked for a number of years to create his own. In contrast to being daily immersed in a colleague-filled office, suddenly Steve was a corporation of one. He felt pretty lonely at times, being, for instance, both CEO and janitor. Out of his experience, however, grew a passion to connect with people just like him. He knew there were self-employed others out there, and he wanted to network with them, to struggle together with what it means to respond to God's call in business and how they might be faithful to Him. As a result, he started a small group called "Jesus and Associates," which a variety of independent contractors and many others also joined. They were a support and encouragement to one another in pursuing their dreams and living out God's call in their lives. Steve created an atmosphere that met the needs of a specific group of people, a group that continued to meet long after he passed the baton to someone else.

A group of wealthy early retirees have gathered around Bob Buford's book *Halftime* to challenge one another on moving from success to significance. Rather than being concerned with acquiring money and possessions, they're discovering how to impact the world for Christ. Some of them would never before have been in the same room together, but their passion to move from riches to relevance has bonded them. Several years and several leaders after they began, they continue to have an incredible effect on both the church and the community.

Jim was one of the guys transformed through the Halftime ministry. He went from not investing much in relationships to making them a priority in his life. Now he is not only a church leader but he also spends significant time in his neighborhood and with his immediate and extended family. He and his wife are committed to using their gifts of hospitality for God's kingdom; in fact, they remodeled their home with the specific purpose of making it a welcoming place for ministry. An atmosphere where people weren't jealous of success freed Jim and others to become good stewards of the resources with which God had blessed them.

WHAT'S GOING ON IN THE ENVIRONMENT AROUND YOU?

Sometimes it's not us but our environment that influences and compels us to thrive. What's going on around you—in your family, your business, your church, your neighborhood, your city? What environmental factors most strongly influence your life?

With Sally, it was her teenage son's hockey practice. Being a hockey mom meant that she was a slave to ice time, committed to chauffeuring her son to the rink at any odd hour (day or night). Ice hockey is serious business in Minnesota, and Sally gathered with other hockey moms whose kids were equally committed. As she got to know them well, she observed that many were unchurched, with no idea who Jesus was. Sally began a mothers-with-teens group just for them, knowing it might be the only setting they'd respond to. Because they knew and trusted Sally, they came; as they tried to figure out who Jesus was in their lives, she found great joy in watching them grow. After three or four years, several of the families joined Sally's church and committed their lives to Christ— largely because she responded to her environment, creating just the right atmosphere for hockey moms.

Todd, a marriage-and-family counselor who's seen the impact of ideal atmosphere, says,

> *I can spend months working on issues with people, trying to get them to change a particular behavior or reconcile a certain relationship, all with little or no results. Then what puzzles me and delights me, but also sometimes frustrates me, is that when these same people are in the right small-group atmosphere they change and grow almost immediately. What I have worked to accomplish for months literally happens in weeks or days.*

You've probably noticed by now that seasons of life, seasons of faith, personal wounds, gifts and passions, and what's happening around us get all mixed together in our lives. They're not easily separated from one another; instead, they interact with and influence one another, painting a composite picture of a person's needs. Nevertheless, all of these stories reflect one thing: Small-group ministries, and small groups themselves, are living, breathing, growing organisms. Again, this means we need to see them as being in an organic growth mode, *not* as something we're building. What all of the aforementioned groups have in common is their sensitivity to what people need, which helps them to move people along the continuum of spiritual growth to knowing Christ in His fullness.

Instead of one small greenhouse whose inhabitants are all in the same atmosphere, we create many greenhouses, adjusting the environment to their precise needs so they can flourish. Instead of temperature, light, moisture, and fertilizer, we must be sensitive to inputs like prayer, the Word of God, support of one another, and the covenant of the group. People may have widely varying outcomes, depending on their specific season of life, season of faith, pains, joys, and giftedness. Increasing the number of atmospheres in your small-group ministry will reach many different kinds of people in and through your church. *The ultimate goal is to have diverse groups available that respond to people's needs rather than have people available to fit into a group's agenda.*

The Bible provides intriguing examples of organic groups. Shadrach, Meshach, and Abednego come to mind; their environment was a foreign land, and while they could have eaten from the king's table, they covenanted together to live in a way that honored the God they served.

Jesus' circle of disciples is another case in point; the individuals were as diverse as a bold Peter, a doubting Thomas, and a greedy Judas Iscariot, but Jesus knew what each needed and responded accordingly.

When David was fleeing Saul, he and his band of mighty men lived in a totally different kind of atmosphere, one of uncertainty and fear, yet they united in the belief that God was at work and in control.

We wonder what atmospheres Paul and Silas, and Paul and Barnabas, left behind them on their missionary journeys.

And we can't help noting the atmosphere of absolute love and affirmation in the Trinity itself.

When we risk the uncertainty of creating atmospheres for a diverse set of people rather than expecting them all to fit into the same atmosphere, we can anticipate the joy of radical outcomes. People begin to think and act differently. Like Steve and Jim, some change their priorities and even their vocation; like Lauren, some change their theology and the application of their belief. Even an entire church's stage of growth can be impacted—Sally's ministry to hockey moms expanded her church's outreach in a whole new way. Diverse cultures, races, and age groups have the freedom to change and grow because the atmosphere they're in is exactly what they need.

Summary Questions

1. How has your ministry responded to the general atmosphere changes that affect small groups today?

   • Do people help create their own groups?

   • What accountability system is in place for group leaders?

   • Do you have a diversity of groups?

2. What kinds of groups could you create that would address people's hurts?

3. Do you know someone who might grow people through a seasons-of-life or seasons-of-faith group?

4. What do you see as the primary difference between (a) allowing people's needs to determine how small groups form and (b) forming them by an established agenda with materials?

CHAPTER FOUR:

PEOPLE DEVELOP IN STAGES

PART ONE: Spiritual Development

When I (David) read the agricultural parables of Jesus, I can't help but smile. They remind me of lessons I learned in that arena myself, starting back when I was in grad school. I was particularly concerned about world hunger at that point in my life, and I entered the field of horticulture and agronomy in hopes of pursuing a career to address the issue. Unfortunately, because I didn't grow up on a farm, I knew very little about agriculture. My undergraduate degrees in biology and chemistry didn't help much either. The humbling truth is I entered the program on probation and started out taking basic courses.

One was called "Weeds 101." It was all about exactly that—weeds—and I was the green kid in the class (no pun intended). Many of the other students were veteran farmers from the Palouse wheat country in eastern Washington State; they all knew a whole lot more about weeds than I did. One field trip—and it really *was* a trip into the fields—stands out in my memory. As we walked together, we learned to identify various weeds. Trying to blend in with the group, I watched closely as one by one these knowledgeable farmers would pull up a weed and ask our prof, "What's this weed, Doc?" He'd identify it as tansy ragwort or curled dock or whatever its scientific name was, and they'd respond by telling him the common name it was known by on the farm. I was starting to get the hang of how this worked, so I boldly uprooted one and said, "Doc, what do you call this?" Before he had a chance to answer, one of the others replied instead. He shot a sidelong look at another farmer, smiled, took the straw he'd been munching from his mouth, and drawled, "Son, we call that wheat."

What could I say? I was a marked man! I had a huge learning curve ahead of me and it showed. Fortunately, I got another chance. At first it wasn't easy to see the difference between weeds and wheat, but I persisted. In fact, I ended up learning more about plants and crops than I imagined possible.

God gives people second chances too—and third, and fourth, and on and on. That's probably why the parable of the sower has such meaning for me. At first reading (see Matthew 13), it seems to illustrate the *one* right kind of "heart soil" needed in order for the gospel to flourish, as if people with any other kind of heart soil will never enter the kingdom of God. If that were true, however, the apostle Paul never would have become a leader of the early Christian church. His heart was hardened to the gospel. He gave assent to Stephen's stoning and was "breathing out murderous threats" against those who were followers of Jesus. But God reached Paul, who became a "light for the Gentiles," a passionate disciple. He and countless others are living testimonies of God's ability to change and develop people.

The power of the Holy Spirit can change our heart soil. God often develops people in stages, and this parable illustrates the stages of *spiritual* development people may go through on their faith journey. There are personal or *sociological* principles that impact our spiritual journey as well; the two work hand in hand as God develops people according to His timing, and understanding *both* is foundational for growing people in small groups.

People don't all develop in the same way at the same time—we're not altogether predictable or alike. When we (like the farmer in the parable) scatter spiritual seed and focus on growing people, we need to remember that even when we may not see it, God is at work, developing them one small step at a time. It's *His* work, not ours. Because He created us all differently, our faith will develop differently too. The uniqueness of our life stories likewise impacts how we mature in our faith.

In the parable of the sower, Jesus illustrates the developmental stages of faith. He was likely referring to a typical field in the Holy Land, and the four types of soil He mentions would have been very familiar to his audience. Jesus knew they would identify with what He was saying about the ground in the fields, but, in addition, He wanted them to examine the soil of their own hearts. Did they recognize their spiritual needs? How ready were they to grow spiritually?

The first seed scattered by the farmer fell on *hard* soil. His listeners knew about the hard-packed soil of the paths around the fields—those paths were the farmer's access to his crops. Baked by the hot sun and trampled on by myriad feet, this soil wouldn't let the seed penetrate and take root, so birds came along and ate it up.

Some people's lives are hard. Battered by disappointment and loss, they steel themselves against being penetrated by anything. They don't want to feel, because they equate feeling with pain. They've learned that life is difficult and have become bitter as a result; they look hard, their language is harsh, and their hearts are callused and closed. When God's Word comes to such people, it can't initially get through; Satan has a heyday, snatching away the very resource that would breathe life to those who are dying but don't know it. It takes the jackhammer of the Holy Spirit to soften that hard soil into fertile ground for the gospel of God's grace.

God did this for Kim, breaking through the hardness of her heart with the power of His love and grace. She'd been a rowdy teenager in high school, and in her early twenties she fell in with a rough crowd— drinking, doing drugs, partying until all hours of the night, living for the next high. It took nearly losing her life in a car accident on a mountain road for God to soften her heart soil. As she lay broken and bleeding in the cold predawn darkness, she cried out, "Is this all there is to life?"

When a neighbor knocked on her door sometime later and invited her to a neighborhood Bible study, she was ready to say yes. The Spirit had softened her, and in the safety of a loving small group, she got to know the Savior who had rescued her. Several years later, I (Betty) stood with her in the front of an auditorium full of Coffee Break leaders. As Kim (now a small-group leader herself) looked out at the sea of faces, she said to me, "They need to know how important they are! There are people like me behind doors everywhere, just waiting for them to knock and invite them to get to know Jesus."

Kate's heart was hard too. She perceived no need for God; in fact, she didn't believe He even existed. She maintained a tidy life as a successful career woman, moving up the corporate ladder and enjoying the good life. Dave, her partner, was a successful engineer and doing the same. They lived together for sixteen years, convinced they were in total control of their lives.

But God had other plans for them. Slowly He chipped away at their defenses. Dave had been raised in a church and was the first to feel the Spirit's nudge. He began to explore his Christian roots, which Kate did not share, and God drew him into a tiny church that embraced him. There he committed his life to Jesus and got involved in a small group. He shared his newfound joy with Kate, but she wanted no part of it. She was a self-made, independent woman, and Christianity was for weaklings. Yet she found herself drawn to the irresistible love of God. "I didn't want to become a Christian," she admitted. "In fact, I fought it every way I knew how. Yet somehow God drew me in, in spite of myself. His love is awesome!"

Together Dave and Kate developed an insatiable hunger for the Word. They credit the believers who walked their spiritual journey with them for accepting them just as they were, allowing them the freedom for their faith to grow in a way that was right for them. "No one challenged or criticized us about our living together," said Kate. "They knew the Holy Spirit would convict us at just the right time, and He did!" Today they're married and reaching out to their non-Christian friends, ministering the same way *their* faith journey developed—slowly, one step at a time, allowing God to work in His timing.

In the parable of the sower, the farmer's seed also fell on *rocky* soil. Unlike with the path, here the seed could penetrate, take root, and blossom. Because it hit rock, though, it blossomed too quickly (from the stress of hitting rock). Unfortunately, because the rocks prevented the roots from going deep enough to flourish, the plant became vulnerable to the intensity of the sun's heat and soon wilted.

Even today, many of the fields in Israel are ringed with stone walls, but not for aesthetic reasons—the fields needed to be de-stoned in order to be fit for planting. The farmers are willing to put forth the effort because they know all too well the danger of plants sprouting too quickly and being scorched by the midday sun. Likewise, people's hearts often need to be de-stoned. Every day we meet those with rocks in their lives that prevent roots from going deep enough to withstand the heat of life's difficulties. When they quickly embrace the Good News, the rocks of childhood abuse or a painful divorce or an abortion or unresolved anger or toxic shame stand in the way of a deeply rooted faith. Then, because their roots were kept shallow, they wilt. People need a place for de-stoning so that their root system isn't blocked and it can penetrate deep into the grace of God.

Sometimes rocky people see Christianity as a quick fix for their problems. In the aftermath of a divorce or the death of a child, they try to use Christ as a Band-Aid to fix what's broken. They embrace Jesus with contagious joy and enthusiasm so strong it can even put longtime believers to shame; they can't stop talking about their newfound faith, to the point that others may find them obnoxious. Then, just as suddenly as their faith erupted, it seems to disappear. They drop out of the church, and we wonder what happened. Often we were simply unaware that there were rocks in their lives needing to be dealt with in order for them to become deeply rooted in God's grace. Once the initial thrill of their newfound faith subsided, they still needed to deal with whatever trauma was interfering with their growth. No one had prepared them for the fact that the Christian walk isn't always easy, and when they became over-whelmed by the stress of the rocks, they fell away.

Chad was one of these people. Though he was raised in a loving Christian home, as a young teenager he rebelled, turned his back on family and faith, and became deeply involved in drugs and alcohol. I (Betty) met him in a small group on discovering our spiritual gifts; he was newly released from a treatment program and on a spiritual high. He raved about his faith, and no matter what our group discussion started with, Chad steered the conversation to his conversion and the miracle of God's love. His energy was contagious—we loved his childlike faith and awe. However, we didn't see his sudden obsession with his faith as the red flag it was. After only a few short months Chad dropped out of our group. Later we discovered he'd been lured back into his old lifestyle and disappeared completely. Underlying his quickly developing faith were the unresolved issues (rocks) in his background, and the heat of life's struggles was too strong for him to endure. We need to be alert when someone's faith is developing in this way, walking alongside them as they address the things that keep them from growing deep and strong.

Then, in the parable, there was the *thorny* soil. Getting rooted wasn't a problem; in fact, plants in thorny soil are deeply rooted . . . but because the soil is rich and pliable, more than just plants can grow in it—thorns and thistles thrive too. The problem comes when thorns and thistles vie for the same air and sunshine, choking out the other plants. People whose faith is like the seed in thorny soil are lured by big houses, new cars, executive offices, impressive titles, lavish vacations, titillating adven-tures, intoxicating power, never-ending drama, and money, money, money. They buy into the world's definition of success. They want Jesus as Savior, but they don't really want him to be Lord of their lives.

Kathy is like that. She has gladly accepted Jesus as her Savior. She prays to Him all the time, usually to ask for more things she doesn't have. But she doesn't want Him to make any demands on her time, and she doesn't want Him to have control of her life. She's too busy decorating her house, building a garden in her backyard, and spending money on her hobbies to find time to be with God. She's too tired to go to church or develop relationships with other believers. She lives her life for herself, in constant pursuit of the next thing to buy or achieve. "God knows my heart," she insists, but she also freely admits she isn't ready to make Him Lord of her life. No doubt God does know her heart, and it grieves Him that she's missing the richness of all He has in store for her.

The final soil, of course, is *good* soil, that which is pliable and ready to receive the seed and grow. These people thrive in a small group because they not only embrace Jesus as Savior and Lord, they also understand the importance of serving others and reaching out to those who don't yet know Christ. They are ready to assume leadership in the church and help equip others to reach those outside the family of God as well.

We will meet people whose heart soil may be any one of these four. We need to reach them right where they are and know that God is able to accomplish things we can't even imagine. Rather than expecting them to be where we want them to be spiritually, we need to accept them just as they are. The process of growing people in small groups is very much like discerning the difference between soils and seeds and wheat and weeds. We can't always immediately tell where people are spiritually. Sometimes we make assumptions we shouldn't: We see the quick blossom of fruit without discerning the rocks beneath that will stunt that burst of growth, or we assume the hardness of the path of someone's life precludes their ever being fertile soil for the gospel. We don't recognize their hostile challenges to Christianity as a cry to understand.

God has made us to work best as a body. We need one another. Some things happen better in a small group than they do when we're alone. The self-made, rugged individualist, no matter where he or she is on the spiritual journey, can go it alone only so long; eventually, something will happen to make it evident that we work best together. (Even the Lone Ranger had Tonto!)

Mike and Gay's story illustrates how God works. Both were born and raised in Christian families, and after their wedding they continued to attend their home church. But ten years into their marriage, Mike stopped attending Sunday worship services. At first, he continued attending mid-week events, but eventually he stopped attending church activities altogether. Gay continued to attend with their daughter, but she was concerned about Mike's pulling away. She missed going to church as a family. She wondered if the situation would ever change. At a crossroads in her life, she decided to pray for a miracle—if it didn't happen, she decided she'd drop out of the church scene herself.

The miracle for which Gay prayed came in the form of an invitation to a small group. She was excited about the opportunity to get involved as a couple; needless to say, Mike was not. Though he agreed to "try it," he did so dragging his feet. The group met on Saturday night and, as Gay tells it, "by Friday I usually had a knot in my stomach. By the time we would leave for our meeting, we often weren't speaking to each other, and I worried about the strain it was putting on our marriage."

Week after week the battle continued. At each meeting Mike stationed himself near the door as if poised to make a quick escape. Finally Gay gave up. One Saturday, after wrestling all day over whether their small group was worth the pain and strain on them as a couple, she decided she couldn't fight it anymore. When Mike came home from work, she informed him of her decision to drop out.

But God was at work in ways Gay didn't see. Much to her surprise, on the same Saturday she surrendered the battle, so did Mike. He told her he wanted to keep going. It was a turning point for both of them. Mike shares his story with candor and insight:

> As Gay mentioned, ten years into our marriage I stopped attending church. The less time I spent at church, the more disconnected I felt. The more disconnected I felt, the more I felt I was not measuring

up to the expectations of other Christians. And it became very easy to stay away from church events.

The invitation to go to a small group was the beginning of a battle; not just between Gay and me, but between us and the devil. Even though I said I would go, in the back of my mind I said "I will go, but I won't like it." Well, we went and continued to go. I continued to give the people in the group every opportunity to kick me out. Gay and I kept arguing, and if we weren't arguing we weren't talking.

I couldn't get away from this small-group thing. Even during the week at work, thoughts of small group came back to me. I would go through my very rational reasons for not going and believe that was good enough. But the thoughts kept coming back daily, even hourly. Frustrated at this, I decided to continue going to the small-group meeting, secretly hoping no one would notice me. It was ironic that Gay and I gave up on the same Saturday. Gay gave up fighting for the small group, and I gave up fighting against it.

Slowly things began to change for me. I started seeing that our small group was different from other Bible studies we had been in. People in this group had problems like me and they were willing to accept me where I was at spiritually. I gradually started to trust the group members and realized that this was a way for me to get connected with the church again. My original excuse of not having enough time didn't seem to matter anymore as I saw how I was being blessed for every minute I was putting into this new opportunity. Our relationship as a couple was also blessed as we spent more time together on our faith journey.

I am a carpenter by trade, and I am thankful to be able to build more than houses. I now feel God's call to build His kingdom and reach out to others.

God was at work—in His time and in His way—with both Mike and Gay. Now they're both active in their church and its small-group ministry. When they were asked to lead a group of young adults, Mike was the first to say yes.

Getting to know and love God is a journey, not an event. A small group offers friends who come alongside, helping us stay on the right path, encouraging us to persevere to the end. Being open to accepting where people are in their spiritual development is important, but it's only part of how God develops people in stages. In the next chapter, we'll show how foundational principles for our spiritual development are integrally related to and intertwined with our personal development as well.

People are complex. They haven't become who they are overnight, and they won't become who they're going to be overnight. All the stuff of life gets mixed together on the road to becoming like Christ. Taking the time to understand the process of growth—spiritually and personally—makes the journey a little easier.

Summary Questions

1. What have you learned about how God develops people spiritually that will help you be a better small-group leader?

2. When people make the assumption that there is only one "right" kind of heart soil, how does that make it difficult for them to connect with others or to grow spiritually? What other kinds of false assumptions could be made about a person's heart soil?

3. There is a danger of becoming judgmental regarding where people are in their spiritual journey. Examine your own attitudes. How can you specifically guard against a judgmental spirit?

4. How can you specifically pray for each person with whom God is challenging you to develop a small-group relationship?

CHAPTER FIVE:

PEOPLE DEVELOP IN STAGES

PART TWO: Principles for Spiritual Development

Jack and Carol were newly married, looking for a place to belong. They were at a curious and cautious point in their faith journey: Each had been through a difficult, painful divorce and had been deeply wounded by harsh criticism and ugly gossip in the churches where they'd been members. Both dropped out for a time as a result. They went through the de-stoning process, and though they'd experienced a measure of personal healing and wanted to start their new marriage with a recommitment to their Christian faith, they were tentative about reconnecting with other people. What they'd endured in the church made them mistrustful of how they would be accepted in their new believing community. They intentionally chose a large church where they could get lost in the crowd, and they decided not to get involved in anything beyond Sunday morning worship.

At the same time, Russ and Rachel, longtime members, were hosting a get-acquainted small group for empty-nester couples who were new to the church. They wanted newcomers to feel welcome; each month they planned a low-key relationship-building time of sharing a meal and playing games together. Noticing that Jack and Carol often seemed to keep to themselves, Russ and Rachel invited them to join the group. The format was simple enough not to be threatening, so Jack and Carol decided to try it. Russ and Rachel genuinely loved people and had wonderful gifts of hospitality and encouragement, making those who came to their home feel relaxed and at ease. For the first time in a very long while, Jack and Carol felt connected with people who cared about them. In the easygoing safety of this small group, a group that respected their need for privacy and accepted them just as they were, they finally found a place to belong. It was God's provision for them at a delicate point on their faith journey, and they found out soon enough how much they would need that little group. Several months after they joined, Jack was diagnosed with colon cancer. The group rallied around them, bringing in meals, visiting the hospital after surgery, and providing transportation for chemotherapy sessions. Jack and Carol were overwhelmed by the love outpouring from their small group. God was not only developing their faith in Him but using His family to develop them personally as well.

Sociological Growth Principles

The stories of faith development we've shared in chapters 4 and 5 are colored by each person's personal and sociological development as well as the growth of their faith. The two cannot be separated. We all experience both faith stages and life stages; sometimes they coincide and develop neatly together and sometimes they don't, but they always impact each other. As we introduced in chapter 3, the sociological principles that underlie the process of people's growth build on one another, beginning with the principles of belonging and support, then moving to the principles of learning retention, life transformation, accountability, experimentation, risk-taking, synergy, decision-making, and problem-solving.*

These are the foundation for all successful small-group models, the glue that holds them together. When we both understand the principles

---

The People Together series of principle-based small-group-training workshops for leaders and managers is available through Faith Alive Christian Resources by calling 1-800-333-8300 or by accessing their Web site: (*www.faithalivechristianresources.org*).

and see what life stages people are in, we're better able to identify the heart soil of our group members and ascertain where they are on their journey of faith. We are also able not only to point them to the kind of group that best meets their needs, but to better discern where they need to be challenged to grow.

These core sociological principles broadly correspond to the different kinds of heart soil we find in people. The principles work together as God develops them so that they first claim Jesus as *Savior,* then as *Lord* of their lives. As they grow they learn the importance of *servanthood* and eventually see God's call to *leadership,* which starts the cycle all over again within the community. In other words, they develop in stages. When growing people (not programs) is our small-group priority, and we start with where they are, not where we want them to be, being sensitive to God's developing them in stages makes sense.

The Principle of Belonging

For most people (like Jack and Carol), both their personal and spiritual development starts with finding a place to belong. All of us need to belong somewhere, whether or not we want to admit it. God is a relational God—Father, Son, and Holy Spirit—and He made us to live in relationship as well. Granted, there are probably some self-sufficient hermits out there, perfectly content with being cut off from society, but what a small world they inhabit! Can you picture living in an environment limited to what you know and who you are, never experiencing the richness of the family of believers, missing the magnificent diversity God has created? (For extroverts like the two of us, this is especially difficult to imagine.)

Belonging is a basic need, foundational in small groups. Before we can do anything else in a small group, we need to feel we belong—this is where the curious and cautious begin their faith journey. They may be miles away from God and still want a place to belong and be accepted by others. Some people never grow spiritually because they have never felt accepted into God's family. A small-group ministry that takes into account various points on various spiritual journeys will need to begin here—with groups that help people feel welcomed and safe.

Remember the story of Jeff, the non-Christian who wanted to have a Bible study with his Christian colleagues in downtown Minneapolis? Jeff was at the "belonging" place in his life. He admitted up front that he wasn't ready to get involved in church, yet he was ready to get to know a bunch of admirable guys at work, so he invited them to a study. When they started, he wasn't sure he wanted a relationship with Jesus, but he wanted to have a relationship with them. Because the soil of his heart was soft and fertile, he built relationships with them, studied God's Word, and soon committed his life to Christ as well.

Jeff's story didn't begin with a downtown small group; God was at work before that. The very guys he invited had long been praying for him; well before Jeff was ready to receive Jesus as his Savior, his friends prayed that he would. God heard and answered those petitions.

Jeff's story doesn't end there either. Five years later, at a weekend retreat for dads, a man named Bill became a Christian. Can you guess who led him to take that step of faith? It was Jeff. As Jeff found a place to belong, he led others to belong as well.

The Principle of Support

Jeff quickly moved beyond just belonging to find support and much more in his small group. Jack and Carol also moved beyond just belonging: In their newfound friendships, they also experienced loving support, daring to trust God again because of what the group modeled for them. After a year of battling cancer, Jack died. The group was there for Carol: They assisted her with funeral arrangements, sat by her side, cried with her, and prayed with her. They brought in food and helped her deal with the mundane details of everyday living. They quietly supported her in every way they knew how.

Carol continued to attend the group alone. Then, only a few months after Jack's death, she was diagnosed with breast cancer. Her group continues to walk with her through this journey as well—loving her, being there for her, and uplifting her.

Support and belonging often go hand in hand. People start by thinking they just want relationships but then realize they need much more— they need to share their lives with others. They long for community, a place to take off their masks and be accepted for who they are, warts and all. Support groups provide an added depth of relationship, allowing people who are struggling in a specific area to hear from others who are also struggling. Together they grow and learn from one another; they pray for each other and walk through trials side by side. Support groups are a common ground where people feel safe because the others truly understand what they're going through.

Susan started out looking for a place to belong and also be supported, but she certainly didn't want it to be in church. She wasn't even sure God existed, and if He did, she certainly didn't feel any need for Him in her life. What she did need, though, was connection with other struggling mothers of teenagers. She joined a Mothers-of-Teens small group, being frank about having zero faith in God or the church, in which she'd seen so many people hurt. Her heart was hard and it showed. Only the power of the Holy Spirit and the grace of God could break up the soil of her heart.

He did just that, but not in a way anyone would have anticipated. After only two weeks of meeting with her small group, Susan's fifteen-year-old son committed suicide. She was devastated. The loss was traumatic not only for her but for the other members as well—they were acutely aware that what happened to Susan could have happened to any of them. They surrounded her with love and support. They walked with her day by day. She cried on their shoulders, and they cried with her. They helped her make ordinary decisions when she was too fragile to think for herself. And God used this tragic loss in her life to become the jackhammer that softened her heart soil so that His love and grace could sink in deeply.

The principles of support and belonging are basic to developing people, and support and belonging happen best in a small group. People don't need awareness of or desire for God in order to want to belong and be supported. Small groups that help people to belong and that support them in an area of need are wonderful opportunities for believers to reach out to those far from God. Often it's at this stage of people's spiritual growth, when they're accepted and embraced just as they are, that they first become open to the Good News and accept Jesus as their Savior. Like Jeff, and like Susan, they acknowledge their need for His grace and take the first halting steps on their spiritual journey to becoming like Christ.

THE PRINCIPLE OF LEARNING RETENTION

In addition to finding that a small group is a place to belong and be supported, people discover that they remember more and learn better in a group than when they're alone. Did you know that on average, people remember 5 percent of what they hear, 10 percent of what they see, 25 percent of what they read, 55 percent of what they discuss, 65 percent of what they create with others, and a whopping 95 percent of what they teach others? This means leaders will almost always remember more than their group members do. Even so, leaders can increase members' learning retention simply by making their group interactive, so that everyone invests in what the group learns and each person becomes both a learner and a teacher.

Remember Kate, the atheist God grew into a devoted disciple? She developed an insatiable hunger for His Word, and she had a million questions as she read her Bible. It was in a small group that she wrestled with the truths of Scripture and applied them to her life. It was the power of the Holy Spirit and the power of learning together that cemented God's Word in her heart.

THE PRINCIPLE OF LIFE TRANSFORMATION

Somewhere along the line, people reach an "aha moment" and experience the transforming power of the Spirit in their lives. They move beyond accepting the truth of God's Word in their head and transfer it to their hearts.

Ellie's life was transformed by a small group called "Bible 101." She'd attended church and listened to sermons every week for years and years, yet somehow, for her, the teaching never got beyond head knowledge. A highly analytical woman, much more thinker than feeler, Ellie often appeared cool and aloof to those around her. Though she knew biblical truths in her head, they didn't connect with her heart.

This changed when she joined a small group that wrestled with these truths together. There she not only embraced scriptural teachings, but they also radically changed her, and people couldn't believe the difference. She went from "cool and aloof" to "on-fire and engaging." She opened her home to people, inviting them warmly and enthusiastically, excited about interacting with them and sharing her faith.

I (David) heard through a friend about the change in Ellie and invited her to my office to find out what was going on in her life. She picked up the Bible sitting on the table next to her and held it up. "Have you ever read this thing?" she demanded. "You can't believe what's in here!" I couldn't help but laugh; I assured her that, yes, I did know what's in there. Then I invited her to tell me what she was learning. Starting in the Old Testament and moving through the teachings in the New Testament, she bubbled with excitement. I realized that God was using her small group to help her understand His Word for the first time, and it was transforming the way she viewed the world. The soil of her heart was rich and ready to receive what He had in store for her.

THE PRINCIPLE OF ACCOUNTABILITY

Becoming accountable to one another is a logical next step after people's lives are transformed by the Holy Spirit. As people in a small group feel accepted for who they are and supported by people who care about them, and as they learn and grow together so that their lives are transformed, they recognize they need help to make the changes they desire. They say, "Hold me accountable for what I say I'm going to do." They've moved from knowing Jesus as Savior to a deep desire to make Him Lord of their lives.

Our (David's) church's fathering team emphasizes accountability because we know how easy it is for us to let the pressures of our jobs and other demands pull us away from our desire to be the dads God wants us to be. We use chalk-talks and meet in huddles, making game plans for our families. Every week we come back to the group and each guy gives himself a gold, silver, or bronze medal or ribbon as we share how well we did at living up to the goals we set for ourselves for being a good husband and a good dad.

Tom was one of the guys in our fathering group. He joined us at a very painful point in his life: After years of success in the corporate world, living on the fast track of a growing company and making big money, Tom's company cut him out, accused him of fraud, and fired him. Everything he'd invested his life in was shattered. But God used that traumatic event to get his attention. He realized that the deceitfulness of wealth and the lure of a "better life" had left him all alone and far from where God wanted him to be. He repented, rearranged his priorities, and got involved in our fathering group.

I remember when Tom asked us to hold him accountable for turning off the TV during breakfast so he'd be available for his family. Sounds like a small step, doesn't it? For a guy addicted to the morning news and living life in the fast lane, choosing to put his family first was a big deal. He knew he'd need his small group to hold him accountable, to ask him whether he'd done it, before he'd make the change. We prayed with Tom as he set his goal, promising to continue to support him. The next week, when we asked him how it went, he had an amazing story to tell. The very first day he turned off the TV, his four-year-old daughter got out of her chair, climbed into her daddy's lap, and said, "Oh, I get it, Dad! It's you and me time now, right?" Tom's little decision to turn off the TV and the guys who held him accountable to do it have had a big impact on his relationship with his little girl. That's the power of what accountability can mean in a small group, helping us make the kinds of changes we know God wants us to make.

The Principle of Experimentation

As we see how God blesses us when we make Him the Lord of our lives, we become more open to experimenting with new behaviors and developing our gifts and talents. The principle of experimentation says we're more likely to do this with a supportive small group cheering us on than when we're on our own.

Tom's decision to turn off his TV in the morning for quality time with his little girl was just the beginning of his decision to make Jesus the Lord of his life. As he continued to put God first, he became not only a better dad and a better husband, he also used his talents and gifts in a new way. Instead of building a personal financial empire, he volunteered his skills and insights to benefit his church. He led a major building campaign and set up systems and structures for responsible stewardship of the resources God had entrusted to them. Because Tom had been a victim of corporate greed, he was especially careful to lead this capital campaign with honesty and integrity. He experimented with using his gifts in a way that was totally beyond his experience, and God blessed both Tom and the church he served.

THE PRINCIPLE OF RISK-TAKING

Closely associated with the principle of experimentation is the principle of risk-taking. Risk-taking also happens more readily with the support of a small group than when we're all alone.

Ann, who understands this firsthand, credits her group for her getting involved in missions in a new way. A strong, honest, straightforward woman who'd built a loyal clientele as a successful attorney, Ann embodied her highly competitive family's motto, "It's a sin to lose." But her thriving practice crumbled and so did she after a series of ugly confrontations cost Ann her job and left her broken and unsure of herself. At that point she became involved in a small group on basic spiritual disciplines. At the start, Ann freely admitted she'd never prayed out loud before. Because of her openness and honesty with God and her group, she grew in her faith by leaps and bounds.

As she matured spiritually, she was challenged by the question, "What's your passion and purpose in life?" She'd never been asked that before, and she realized she really wanted to be involved with children—

especially with missions for children. With the encouragement of her group, she became involved in helping her congregation sponsor needy children through World Vision. Family after family responded to her passion and partnered with Ann in sponsoring children whose families were being devastated by AIDS in Africa. Eventually Ann became an assistant to her missions pastor, using her legal abilities to help the cause of Christ all over the world. God used both her life experiences and the development of her faith to grow her into a beautiful servant of Jesus.

Another small group of women in the workplace wanted their faith to make a difference every day, and they covenanted with one another to do so. One woman risked something as simple as praying this prayer daily: "Lord, if you could use me today in some way, I am really willing to follow you." Week after week she shared with her group the specific ways God used her, either in big or small ways, when she earnestly prayed that prayer. It was almost frightening to her. "How far is this thing going to go?" she asked her leader, awed at how God was answering her simple prayer.

All these stories and countless others like them illustrate the incredible ways people grow and develop when no matter what their circumstances, they get rid of the rocks in their lives, choke out the world's definition of success, and sink their roots deeply into the grace of God. They move from knowing Jesus as Savior and Lord to becoming His servants, using the gifts He's given them in ways that grow others in their faith as well.

THE PRINCIPLE OF SYNERGY

Many of the people whose stories we've shared experienced a synergy in their small group that they didn't experience when they were alone. Simply stated, synergy is when the whole is greater than the sum of its parts, or when one plus one plus one equals five instead of three. Synergy, which becomes real as the body of believers works together, is readily seen in task forces and teams focused on a specific goal. People's commitment and motivation is greater in teams where they can contribute according to their gifts and talents.

I (David) saw synergy as the key principle at work in getting our men's ministry to take off. I inherited it when I first came to the church, and for several years George and I ran the whole thing together. We sponsored a men's breakfast each month that averaged about forty or fifty guys, but we knew that for the size of our church we weren't maximizing our potential.

So we prayed together and with God's guidance worked to develop a new vision for our men's ministry. We were done being a one-man-band plus one. We planned a vision retreat and invited the men of our church to join us, praying God would raise up the ones He was preparing to lead that ministry. He did. A small group of guys were looking for a challenge, guys with a variety of gifts and passions. I told them how much we needed help, and they eagerly got involved. Mike helped me redesign the entire ministry. Ward added the gift of administration. Todd, a gifted musician, pitched in too, as did eight other men. Together we formed a team and over a five-year period grew the ministry so that the men's breakfast began to average more than three hundred guys each quarter, and all kinds of small groups were launched as well. God used the synergy of men with gifts of vision, administration, music, helps, and other gifts, guys who got together and gave their best to create something that served others. Then they moved from serving others to providing leadership as well.

THE PRINCIPLES OF DECISION-MAKING AND PROBLEM-SOLVING

When God moves people in their spiritual development to the point of leadership, He especially wants them to work together. Leadership is not to be taken lightly, nor is it to be taken too seriously. But leaders who isolate themselves from the wisdom of others do not serve in the best possible way.

Some of the best church-leadership teams (and other task teams) understand the principles of decision-making and problem-solving. In making decisions regarding strategy and development, or even to resolve conflict or other problems, using the best gifts and input of those qualified nets better decisions than those made individually.

One of the most valued teams in our (David's) church is the LifeKeys team. We help people identify their gifts and talents and passions and get them connected in a ministry that fits with how God wired them. I developed the spiritual-gifts aspect of our training and had the overall vision for how we could work together. Jane Kise, who has the gift of writing, and Sandra Hirsh, who is nationally known as a Myers-Briggs (Personality) Type Indicator expert, each contributed in their area of expertise. We developed a seminar and training materials that could be used in a wide variety of settings. As LifeKeys grew, we added other trainers who also lead LifeKeys seminars around the country. LifeKeys is now an international ministry, but only because the Holy Spirit put together a group of people who worked in synergy *and* problem-solved to make what we did more effective. Over time, we refined LifeKeys so that churches around the world can benefit from the work God allowed us to create.

As mentioned earlier, I (Betty) was given the responsibility of developing a small-group strategy that would serve an entire denomination. Though I attended a wide variety of training seminars and explored many models, I never considered making the final decision regarding what would work best by myself. That kind of determination needed to be owned by everyone who would be involved in consulting with churches about small groups and training small-group leaders.

In addition, I always debriefed what I was learning with a circle of trusted leaders whose insights I respected. After experimenting with several approaches for small groups, I asked these small-group representatives for their input. Their endorsement and full support were vital for any strategy to work. We wrestled with the pros and cons of principle-based ministry and how to implement it. We had invested heavily in another strategy, so change wouldn't be easy. Eventually, one wise leader suggested, "Why don't we just try it for a year and see what happens?"

The group agreed. We would work with it a year or two and then reevaluate. That was eight years ago, and we're more convinced than ever that the decision we made together was a good one.

These principles work in more than just task- and leadership-team situations. They're effective in other small groups as well, especially those whose purpose is to build authentic community.

Rick was a member of that kind of small group, a deeply spiritual group that spent a lot of time praying for one another. One of their primary purposes, in fact, was to help one another discern God's guidance about where they were going in their lives. Rick had made a decision to move to a different state and start a ministry there; he was excited about it, ready to pull up his family and leave, and the group had all been praying and supporting him in his decision. Then one day, as they were breaking up, Dave, a group member, shared with Peggy (another), "I just don't feel very good about this decision." She froze in her tracks— she had the same misgivings. A third, Harold, said that he'd had a mental picture of a half-built ship being launched out and destined to sink in the harbor. As difficult as it was, the three of them turned around, sat down with Rick, and shared their concerns. "We're not trying to block you or hold you back," they said, "But the three of us, from different perspectives, just feel like this isn't the right timing. This isn't the right way."

Obviously Rick was taken aback at their seemingly sudden change of support, but he promised to pray about their insights. In the end, he delayed his decision and as a result became an important part of another ministry in the city he was already in. Because his heart soil was rich and fertile, he trusted God's leading through his community of believers. Because he trusted his friends, he made a better decision than he might have if he'd made it on his own. God used his gifts in leadership to serve an even broader community of believers than he'd previously envisioned.

Fluidity and Flexibility

God develops people in His own time and in His own way; these sociological principles and stages of spiritual development are simply pieces to help us see where He's at work. Though these wonderful concepts for growing people in small groups seem precise and tidy, we need to be honest with you: They're only tools. People aren't always neat and tidy; small groups can be pretty messy. And though the different soils illustrate the different stages of faith development, and the sociological principles illustrate the different stages of personal development, they don't always neatly coincide. People are organisms, not organizations: They're fluid and highly flexible; they change when we least expect it; they value freedom. This is good! This is how God created us to be! We celebrate this!

Life isn't linear or logical, and neither is the development of our faith. We accept Christ and make a huge leap forward. We have a broken engagement and take three steps back. We get a job we love and move five steps forward. We get married to the "perfect mate" and move ahead more. Then we suffer a miscarriage, lose a job, encounter illness, and come to grips with the fact that life isn't always easy—actually, it's rarely easy—and whether its circumstances move us forward, backward, or not at all really depends on each individual.

No individual and no small group develops the same way as another. Both their seasons of faith and their seasons of life experiences will be different. Each has its own timing, its own life cycle. Nevertheless, at some point both individuals and small groups can undergo change, moving around the circle of principles. Not only individuals in the group, but the group itself begins to mature. Leaders need to be tuned in to both factors (spiritual and personal) and both realms (individual members and the group as a whole).

The power of these principles is seen as God develops a person's spiritual formation. Danell was first introduced to principle-based small groups when she accepted the position of being a small-group representative in the Southwest U.S. and attended leadership training. As David Stark explained each principle and how they all work together, she paid careful attention and took lots of notes. He showed her how a person doesn't have to know Christ in order to want a place to belong and be supported, but somewhere along the way God begins to work, and that person accepts Jesus as Savior. The principle of learning retention kicks in as he or she develops an insatiable thirst for God's Word. Then the principles of transformation and accountability come into play as he or she understands biblical truths and makes Jesus Lord of his or her life. Subsequently, as God grows a person, he or she begins to want to give back, to experiment with spiritual gifts and passions, to work in synergy with others, to take risks, solve problems, and make decisions with others. He or she wants not only to serve but to develop leadership gifts as well.

I (Betty) watched as Danell soaked in what David was teaching, unable to read what she was thinking, aware that it was all new to her. Finally I asked, "What do you think, Danell? Does this make sense?" She smiled and nodded. Then she pointed to the circle of principles and their parallel with spiritual development: "This is me. This is my story. This is how God developed me. I know it's true because it happened to me."

The wonder is that these principles allow us to know not only where individuals are but where the whole church is and also where pockets or groups within the church are. Where do you see your men? What about your youth group? Your staff? Young marrieds? Empty-nesters? What kinds of small groups are needed to reach people in your church and your community, nudging them to where God is leading?

You can actually discern a small group's level of maturity by seeing what small-group principle they (as a whole) are working on. Some will never move beyond the principles of support and belonging, because that's all they were ever intended to do. That's okay! Celebrate the fact that they're doing exactly what they said they would do: give people a place to feel comfortable and accepted. Not all groups need to experience all the principles or experience them in the same way.

However, a small group on spiritual disciplines, for instance, that doesn't move beyond support and belonging is in deep trouble—it isn't living up to what it said it would become. Those groups will need to evaluate themselves and ask, "Is this what we said we would do? Why aren't we becoming more spiritually intimate with God and with one another? What steps do we need to take to accomplish the goals we set for ourselves?"

Take a deep breath now and remember this: *God* develops people. *We* just need to love them. It really is that basic. Knowing the stages of spiritual and sociological development (for people and for small groups) is a wonderful tool to make us more effective as leaders, but it truly is God who provides the growth. We don't need to get everything right or feel completely responsible for all the outcomes. We simply need to follow the law of love and set people free to develop as God leads them. So tuck away this information, celebrate the journey God allows us to take with Him, and experience the freedom that comes when we let Him develop people His way.

Summary Questions

1. What have you learned about the importance of understanding the principles involved in an individual's (and a group's) personal development?

2. What principle(s) do you see predominantly at work in your current small group(s)?

3. How can you use these principles to be more aware of what people need?

4. What challenges do you see for your small-group ministry and for you as a small-group leader?

WHAT ARE SMALL GROUP PRINCIPLES, AND HOW DO THEY FACILITATE SPIRITUAL TRANSFORMATION?

Principles of Small Group Ministry

Diagram taken from *Launch and Lead Your Small Group Ministry,* Faith Alive Christian Resources. Used by permission.

CHAPTER SIX:

GROW WHAT'S BLOOMING

Les and Amy, a young couple in a small New England church plant, have blossomed because an insightful pastor and small-group leader freed them to use their gifts in a way that fits how God designed them. This gifted husband and wife could easily have been used in a variety of ministry settings. Les is a former captain in the U.S. Marine Corps, with obvious leadership gifts. Amy runs her own business and has tremendous marketing and promotional ideas. In a small church plant, every person is desperately needed; their leaders faced a natural temptation to use Les and Amy in areas of *need* rather than where they would best *thrive*. Avoiding that temptation and encouraging them to work in their areas of giftedness, doing what God designed them to do, benefited this little church in big ways.

Les has a passion for connecting with people. He wanted to get to know those inside the church as well as reach out to those in the community. As an avid outdoorsman, he wondered if there was a way to combine his love for people with his love of hunting and fishing. His pastor saw what was blooming and connected him with the Sportsperson's ministry of Kelloggsville Church in Kentwood, Michigan. Les attended a conference sponsored by Kelloggsville and came home full of ideas on how to begin an outreaching sports ministry—he couldn't wait to get started!

That was only a couple of years ago. Since the sporting club began, more than two hundred community people have come to this tiny church to attend one or more of the events. It's primarily a relationship-building small group, so the meetings are low-key in nature. They serve as a bridge for people from the congregation to connect with those in the community, many of whom wouldn't normally walk through the door of a church building. Les leads the meetings and activities with contagious enthusiasm and effortless energy because he's doing what God designed him to do.

Amy has found her niche too, and it's been a huge asset to Les and the sporting club: She uses her business background with her experience and expertise in advertising to help get the word out; her flyers, signs, and newspaper ads for the various events are eye-catching, clever, and compelling. Together Les and Amy make a great team for this ministry. Because they're serving in their areas of interest and passion, they need only minimal support from the church leadership. There's been no forced fit or awkward role-filling, since they're doing what's natural to them. They were freed to grow what was already blooming, and God has blessed their ministry greatly.

God orchestrates and originates the vision for small groups. We deeply believe that He knows what's best for every church, and we constantly ask, "What is God up to in the various parts of our congregation?" In addition, the Creator knew exactly what He was doing when He put certain gifts and talents and passions into laypeople; partnering with Him as He develops people in small groups is an awesome privilege. Seeing Him at work and being His hands, feet, and voice so we grow what's blooming builds the church of Jesus Christ and brings joy to God's heart and ours. People like Les and Amy personify the effectiveness of small-group ministry when they're allowed to blossom in ways God designed.

Historically the church hasn't always trusted "ordinary people." It took the Protestant Reformation to bring God's Word and God's work back to the masses. Johann Gutenberg's fifteenth-century invention of the printing press was instrumental in putting the Bible into the hands of the common person for the first time; previously, the Word of God was entrusted to the clergy alone. Paul, however, includes *all* believers in the gifts God gives (Romans 12:4–6), and using those gifts begins with the challenge not to be conformed to the pattern of this world, "but be transformed by the renewing of your mind" (v. 2). Renewing your mind enables you to discern God's perfect will, and that is done "with sober judgment, in accordance with the measure of faith God has given you" (v. 3). We're all parts of one body, each with different gifts, and God wants us to fully use what He's given us.

The Reformation began the shift into empowering the laity to do God's work—ministry in the name of Jesus—and that shift continues today. One of the vehicles for facilitating this empowerment is small groups. In the twenty-first century, the small-group movement carries on the challenge of freeing laypeople to blossom, continuing the fulfillment of the prophecy:

> *I will pour out my Spirit on all people. Your sons and daughters will prophesy, your young men will see visions, your old men will dream dreams. Even on my servants, both men and women, I will pour out my Spirit in those days, and they will prophesy. (Acts 2:17– 18, from Joel 2)*

The Holy Spirit is igniting a spirit of revival in the church, using the passions, dreams, and ideas God has laid on people's hearts, gifting them to realize and accomplish them.

Every congregation and every group of people has been given a set of gifts and talents. From those gifts and talents God calls out a different kind of ministry in each congregation. Rather than prescribing a certain kind of group for everyone—which is a mechanistic approach—those entrusted with oversight must discern the kinds of small groups God intends for a particular church in two ways: through intentional, constant prayer, and through keeping their fingers on the pulse of the community around them. By listening to God's voice and interpreting the atmosphere—by asking what God is up to all around us—small-group managers can usually discern what would best fit their congregation.

Providing small-group oversight includes creating a climate for leaders' gifts to thrive. Sometimes this means smoothing the way for them when they bump up against the "system." They may have had wonderful dreams and ideas for beginning a small group, but then found that the time and energy it took to get permission to begin was so complicated and exhausting that they gave up on the whole process. Churches that are permission-giving within the boundaries of their vision repeatedly find that the Holy Spirit releases within laypeople an enormous vision that managers can then empower in ministry.

On the other hand, there are make-me-an-offer kinds of leaders. God is working in them, and they're open to His leading, but they need someone to define a small-group dream for them and invite them to participate in pursuing it. In organic small-group ministry, there will always be a balance between groups that come from the passions and gifts of laypeople and those that join out of a discerned need because the small-group manager interpreted the community.

With the focus on growing people, it's a new day for small groups. We need a process that (a) takes seriously how to draw out the dreams and passions God lays on the hearts of His people and (b) provides an avenue to reach the community they serve. We need to empower leaders in the ministries God meant for them to be in.

Again, a model-based paradigm for small groups is no longer effective as a comprehensive strategy because it presumes one-size-fits-all thinking. Models promote one kind of covenant, one set of goals, and one kind of evaluation for one set of outcomes. Tapping into people's passions is often a distant second to the priority of promoting an agenda. Rather than saying, "Tell us your passions and we'll help you use your gifts in small groups," models say, "This is *our* passion; if it's yours too, then come be a part of our small groups." Models do work in specific settings, and they will always be an important *aspect* of a comprehensive small-group strategy. But they are most effective if they are part of a larger empowering strategy that focuses first on how God is working in the lives of individuals.

God created people too uniquely for all of us to respond in the same way. It doesn't work to try to fit a gazillion different pegs—with all our shapes and sizes—into the same hole. Not every leader looks alike, and not every small-group purpose will be the same. There are at least three compelling reasons to have the passions of laypeople involved in your church's small-group design.

First, people's passions are often connected to the talents God has given them. One easy way to find out where their abilities lie is to have them share the kinds of small groups they would like to embrace. In what kinds of ministries would they like to engage? Most of the time (though not always), there's a direct connection between a person's passion and his or her talents.

Second, as we have seen, people own what they help create. One of the ways to get high buy-in with the small groups you're designing— and to the ministry as a whole—is to allow people to create from their own passions the types of small groups they want to be involved in. This engages the deepest parts of their being. They actually have a vision for the group, which builds commitment and a long-term perseverance when things don't go exactly as planned or when there are problems that need to be addressed as the groups are launched.

Third, laypeople know how to design things that other laypeople will embrace better than clergy do. As a pastor myself, I (David) hate to admit it, but we can be woefully out of touch with what people really need. When pastors sit back in their offices and try to design experiences in which ordinary people would want to invest, we aren't in the shoes of the people we're trying to engage. I've worked with principle-based small groups more than a dozen years now, and I've seen over and over that when laypeople design out of their own passions, the small groups are more spiritually focused than anything I as a pastor would have ever conceived.

Let me share a story to illustrate. A few years ago I was invited to speak about small groups at a church council meeting. What I didn't know at the time was that no one on the council had any interest in small groups, nor did they have any intention of starting them. I was invited solely as a token gesture and show of support for two very discouraged associate pastors who *were* interested. The council wanted to encourage these two associates, who were trying to hold the church together after the senior pastor's departure almost a year earlier.

It's probably a good thing I didn't know everything that was going on. I did notice, however, that most people weren't paying much attention to me, which indicated that I needed to up the energy ante and ignite a little interest in starting small groups. I asked everyone to take out a piece of paper and answer a few questions, questions I ordinarily use to get potential leaders to think about designing groups. The first was, "What kind of small group would you change your schedule to be a part of? What would its purpose be?" Then I asked, "What community do you want to serve with this group, either inside or outside the church?" Finally, "What results do you want to get as a result of being a part of this group?"

After giving them a few minutes to think, I started writing their ideas on the whiteboard. One man said, "You know, I've always loved cooking. I'm kind of a gourmet chef, and I'd really like to have a small group who made different dishes from countries all over the world—Pakistan, Peru, India, wherever. We would eat together and rotate whose house we met in. We could do some research to find a prayer that came from that country, and, as we ate, discuss what that prayer meant and how it might have been important to that culture. We could end by spending time praying for that country."

Then another gentleman offered his idea. "You know, the number one need in our community is the Neighborhood Watch program, because we have a lot of crime occurring right around the area of our church location. I think we ought to be the place that calls the Neighborhood Watch groups together. We could become the center for protecting those around our church."

A third man said, "I'm a person who really wants to do an in-depth, commentary-based Bible study. I love to dig into the background and history of the text of the Bible, and I'd like to be in a group with others interested in the same thing."

Fifteen minutes later, the dreams for nine different kinds of small groups had been shared. The room was buzzing; people were ready and eager to hear what I had to say about the process. More than that, one guy finally blurted out, "When exactly are we going to start this small-group ministry?" A simple exercise had tapped into the passions of an entire church council. They went from passive resistance to active involvement, and the ideas generated were far more creative than anything a pastor or a group of paid staff could have planned. Igniting the passions of others is powerful.

It can also be scary! Some people equate lack of control with being out of control, but the two are not the same. Growing what's blooming is important, but this isn't done without boundaries. As we stated earlier, all the creative energy of forming new groups needs to fit inside the nesting vision of the small-group ministry: it's *not* anything goes. Once the management team (or leadership team or coaches) defines the nesting vision, each group leader commits to being accountable to that vision in the following ways:

(1) *Their small group will fit within that vision.*
(2) *They will maintain an ongoing relationship with a coach/manager as the group grows.*
(3) *They will honor any guidelines the church requires for choosing curriculum or study material for their group.*

When empowering others to pursue God's dreams seems like you're losing control, remember that you really aren't. You're setting parameters that are broad enough to dream as God intends but tight enough to keep heresy out. All small groups need to be part of the process of growing people so they become more like Christ.

Control is an illusion anyhow—if it feels like you're losing control, remember: you probably never had it in the first place. If we don't allow people some freedom, they will find a way to sabotage attempts to control them. *Responsible freedom will not result in chaos.*

The business community is familiar with a concept called "chaos theory," which developed when a mathematician entered non-linear equations into a computer, then allowed the machine to plot whatever happened. He expected a mess at the end because non-linear equations don't have patterns to them (that we know of). Much to his surprise, however, he ended up not with chaos but with what are now called "strange attractors," which formed fractals, or non-linear repeating patterns. In the plant world, for example, ferns and other beautiful designs illustrate these patterns.

Why talk about chaos theory? Because though we fear chaos will happen when we let go of control and allow people to shape small groups in their own way, it won't. Though we fear there will be nothing positive or redemptive happening in the process, we're wrong. The small-group nesting vision is the equation that surrounds the overall ministry. Within that parameter, we encourage people to dream as wildly as possible. God blesses our letting go. Instead of chaos, we end up with beautiful patterns of small groups where His Spirit is at work, very much like the fractals described in those non-linear equations.

A helpful process for helping people dream God's dreams and focus on designing a small group is found in four simple questions:

(1) *What small-group purpose would you change your schedule to be part of?*
(2) *Who's your target audience?*
(3) *What are the desired results?*
(4) *What kind of group is it?*

Behind the first question is the premise that people are busy enough. We're not asking them to *add* something to their schedule but to *change* their schedule so this small group is a priority. Think big. Small groups don't necessarily have to be held inside the church building. In fact, more and more we see the importance of designing groups that connect both inside and outside the church. Some of them might even be totally out in the community—held in a business setting or someone's neighborhood.

Jane took the design questions seriously when she started a small group. In answering the first question, she decided she would definitely change her schedule to be part of a group of early-morning walkers. She'd gained an extra twenty pounds during her parenting years, and now that she was an empty-nester, she wanted to get in shape. She had blood pressure problems also, and her doctor had encouraged her to fit regular brisk walking into her daily routine. She figured there were probably women like her in the area, and she began making plans to invite others to join her.

That leads us to the second design question: Who's your target audience? In other words, which community do you want to serve with this group? It may include all the women in your church. It may be everybody left at the department store after their most recent downsizing. It may be after-school soccer moms. It may be everyone who commutes daily on the downtown train or bus. Your target audience can be as general or as specific as you want it to be. In our (David's) fathering ministry, we have fathers-of-sons groups, fathers-of-teenage-sons groups, fathers-of-daughters groups, and even fathers-from-a-distance groups for those parenting in a divorce situation or when their kids are in college. Make your audience as broad or as narrow as you choose, but be clear about who you're trying to reach.

Jane's target audience, the community she wanted to serve, was her own unchurched neighbors. She invited three of them to join her, and they did. At 6:00 A.M., four days a week, this loyal foursome dragged themselves out of bed, pulled on their sweats, met at the designated corner, and walked through their neighborhood for fifty to sixty minutes. They laughed at how they looked—there were no pretenses! For Jane, it was a wonderful time of getting to know women she'd barely greeted before.

The third question, What are the desired results? will mean writing down three or four outcomes at the onset and will give the leader something by which to evaluate the group's progress.

Jane's *initial* goal for her walking group was to get in shape; everyone was aware of the goal and agreed to it, and, in fact, all of them lost weight and toned up. But Jane also had two other goals. She wanted to build a relationship with her neighbors, and she wanted to share her faith in Christ. She accomplished both. As these neighbors shared their lives together during those early-morning walks, they became good friends. Jane prayed faithfully for them.

Over time, as they built trust and learned to care for one another, God answered Jane's prayers for a chance to share her love for Jesus. She found little ways to share her own spiritual journey with them, and eventually they actually asked her to lead a Bible study. It was a wonderful time, and Linda was the first to commit her life to Christ. Eventually Jane's husband had a job transfer to another city, and they moved away. But the group continued without her—Linda is leading, and others have joined as well.

As for the fourth question, What kind of group is it? there are four primary types of small groups: being groups, caring groups, learning groups, and working groups.

Being groups are for building relationships and getting to know people. These are the non-threatening places in which non-Christians often first become open to connecting—or reconnecting—with the church.

Caring groups provide support for people with a specific interest or need. Like the grief-support group Janet led, these can also be an entry point at which non-Christians enter the church. Caring groups cover a wide spectrum, from preventive groups (such as preparing for marriage) to support groups (for cancer survivors, those in grief, parenting your preschooler, empty-nesters) to recovery groups for people dealing with addictive behaviors (like AA and other Twelve-Step examples).

Learning groups include Bible study groups and others that have learning as their primary agenda.

Working groups are task-oriented groups that focus on the projects they've undertaken. The praise team in your church may be a working group, similar to groups building Habitat for Humanity homes.

Though most small groups have pieces of all these elements—being, caring, learning, working—what dominates the agenda of the group determines its type. A fifth kind of group is a blend of the others; it has a mixed agenda because no single focus is dominant.

Jane's was a "being" small group. Their primary agenda was walking—getting in shape and losing weight. Though they also wanted to get to know and care for one another, the primary agenda was spending time together and building relationships *while* they got in shape. It was as time passed that their agenda led to another group and another agenda. The Bible study that evolved out of the walking group was a learning group.

Like Jane, Annette designed a small group out of the life stage she was in. Annette had been an interior designer for a number of years but had recently married and was facing the challenges of large-scale change. She felt called by God to walk through this process with others like her, so she created a small group for women in their late forties and fifties with similar situations. She called the group "What Now, What Next?" as in, What would the rest of their life look like? The purpose was to get together and design the next phase of their life. Those attending the group not only forged close friendships, but they also discerned together where God was leading them, learning how to make the next chapter the best it could be.

As Annette developed the group God laid on her heart, He used her creative gifts in a special way. With the help of an artist friend, she wrote creative journals filled with questions that the group used each week. As Annette put it, "It was like I was anointed. I just sat down at the computer one morning and couldn't stop writing. The words just flowed out of me—a plan of exactly what we were supposed to do, the Bible study questions we were supposed to answer, the topics to be covered each week." She was growing what was already blooming in her heart, and God blessed the use of her gifts.

Not only spiritual gifts, but personality, passions, and life experiences determine what kind of group will compel people to change their schedules. Chris is a warm, highly relational extrovert who loves people and has the spiritual gifts of wisdom and encouragement. She could have designed a number of kinds of groups; for instance, she led various small-group Bible studies for several years. Then, at the age of thirty-five, Chris was diagnosed with breast cancer and her whole life was turned upside down. There was no history of breast cancer in her family, nothing that would have indicated she might be particularly susceptible to the disease. After a bilateral mastectomy, reconstructive surgery, and a long bout of chemotherapy, Chris sank into a period of deep depression. God seemed to be just beyond her grasp as day after day she struggled with the dark clouds shrouding her life.

She emerged from that experience with a new hope, a vibrant faith, and a passion for reaching out to others. She also had a clear focus: She wanted to reach women dealing with depression. Chris was now a cancer survivor.

Someone else designing a small group might have naturally pegged her to lead a group for cancer survivors, but that wasn't her passion. Her passion was connecting with women who felt the despair and helplessness of the dark world of depression. She did, and in this niche she became an effective leader, re-illustrating why allowing people to design their own groups out of their gifts, passions, and life experiences honors where God is at work.

Another group that developed out of people's life experiences was "The Dream Team," started by three couples with special-needs children, designed for parents like themselves. They understood the unique challenges of raising a special-needs child and the kind of support that parents and family members needed. Paul and Nan, who had a son with Down's syndrome, started the group, and five years later their son died. It was their small group that stood by their side, mourning with them and supporting them in their loss. These were people who understood the struggles they'd lived with day in and day out. The group's agenda is simple—to pray for one another and share the struggles of their lives together, but those attending say it's been an anchor of support in their lives.

In a similar kind of group, a nurse who understood the stress of daily making life-and-death decisions had a passion for starting a Bible study for other nurses and health care professionals. She had no idea whether anyone else would be interested, but she put a notice in a newsletter for area health care employees and waited to see what would happen. The response was overwhelming: Not only did she start a Bible study in the hospital where she worked but in two other hospitals as well.

These are only a few examples of small groups that grew out of what was already blossoming in people's hearts. As we open the doors to individual dreams and passions, God not only meets the needs of others, sometimes He even uses those groups to birth entire ministries. The Minneapolis fathering ministry began as one small group but has blossomed into six different kinds of fathering groups. One discipleship group for young moms has blossomed into fourteen different discipleship groups. One group for employed moms has expanded to four. God takes the passion of one person and multiplies it over and over. Each of these groups started with the gifts and passions of just one person.

God gives people a unique set of natural talents, spiritual gifts, passions, and life experiences. Although He can use any person in any setting He chooses, there is a pattern and parallel that often accompanies how people are wired and the kinds of small groups they design. People's spiritual gifts often correlate with the kind of group they choose to lead.

Spiritual Gifts and Small-Group Compatibility

Task-oriented small groups are most successful when they're led by people with the gifts of leadership and/or administration. These two gifts are often at the center of the task-group's agenda, facilitating the completion of the work that unites them. Caring and support groups are typically led by people with the gifts of mercy, healing, encouragement, and/or helps. Content-oriented Bible studies, book studies, and spiritual formation studies—learning groups—are most often led by people with the gift of teaching and the gift of shepherding. Sometimes a word of wisdom and a word of knowledge are also involved, but typically leaders with the gift of teaching and/or the gift of shepherding are central to these groups. Relationship-building ("being") groups are usually led by people with the gift of hospitality, the gift of evangelism, or even the gift of shepherding. Again, though there may be overlap and exceptions, these are the gifts most commonly associated with the various kinds of small groups.

Lee had strong leadership gifts and loved getting things done. The small group he wanted to lead was an in-depth Bible study with a twist: He wanted a task component. He worked well with his hands, and he wanted the men in his group to be "doers of the Word, and not hearers only." So in addition to studying the Bible together, Lee and the guys volunteered their services to the single moms in their church. When these moms needed something fixed or moved, they knew whom to call—Lee and his group. It was Lee's gift of leadership and his natural mechanical talent and ability to build things that enabled him to design that group. The members loved the combination of learning and doing, and so did the grateful single moms who benefited from their labor of love.

Bob's small-group design was quite different from Lee's, but it too was determined by both his life circumstances and his spiritual gifts. Bob went through a difficult divorce and felt like he was losing control of his life. He was very angry. He also had the gifts of mercy and encouragement and knew there must be other guys out there like him. He started an anger-management support group that ministered to men struggling with similar issues. Together they looked at what God's Word has to say about anger, and they learned the importance of forgiveness. Eventually

Bob decided to attend seminary in hopes of getting involved with a pastoral-counseling ministry. His life experience and his spiritual gifts were a good fit for the group he chose to start and the effort blossomed into other opportunities as well.

The mother who started a moms-of-teens small group had the gift of shepherding, but she had no idea how God would call her to use it. Then, just two weeks into the start of the group, the world of one member, Susan, came crashing down around her. As mentioned in chapter 5, Susan's teenage son committed suicide. The content curriculum on raising boys, which this dedicated leader had carefully chosen, was pretty much thrown out the window during those early traumatic days and weeks following the death of Susan's son. But God used the steadiness and quiet comfort of this gifted shepherding leader to hold the emotionally fragile group together. She resourced pastors and counselors and others in supportive roles, and God used her gifts and passions to minister to Susan in such a powerful way that Susan committed her life to Christ.

Every spiritual gift has an atmosphere in which it thrives; these stories illustrate only some of them. What's blooming in people's lives may be connected to their spiritual gifts but may also come from a natural talent they have. People's life experiences and the passions God has embedded deep in their soul also contribute strongly to what compels them to reach out and serve others in small groups. We need to do what we can to create an atmosphere that grows what's blooming, thereby freeing people to develop the small groups God has wired them to lead. Remember: *People own what they help create.* When you're free to grow what you're passionate about—within the parameter of the small-group nesting vision—the Holy Spirit is released to perform unique and specific work within your ministry. You will grow what you are meant to grow.

Many years ago, when I (David) first started managing an acre and a half of glass as a greenhouse nurseryman, I visited a man known as the best rose grower in Seattle. As we talked, I asked him, "What would you tell a young guy like me who's just beginning to manage a greenhouse nursery?" I'll never forget his answer—it continues to guide what I do today. He said, "Dave, learn how to grow one or two things well. Because when you learn how to grow one or two things well, you will learn all the principles behind growing everything else."

This rose grower was wise. What he said likewise applies to our small-group ministries. Each ministry—each *group*—is unique, thriving in different atmospheres. Each has its own calling within the community it serves. Each has its own DNA that arises out of the talents and passions of the laypeople God draws to it.

Churches also have a DNA that affects the growth of small groups. Sometimes the soil conditions or spiritual climate in a particular church might make it difficult to grow anything large, so the "plants" produced are dwarfed. In churches like this it isn't easy to persuade people to become Christians or be a part of a small group. Other churches have fertile soil and lush plant life. Anything vital can grow, so the challenge will be to determine what God is blessing, and then prioritize all the opportunities available. Whatever the soil or DNA, the underlying principles that apply to all groups (and all small-group ministries) need our focus as well. The principles combined with the unique small-group DNA will guide managers and leaders in a way that grows up disciples of Jesus.

If you are part of a smaller church, you may wonder how this applies to you. Please remember this: As you open up to the idea of dreaming dreams, you may not be able to offer everything that laypeople want because you will not have the resources in place to support all those dreams. You may need to focus on a few that seem to make the most sense and for which you have the most resources. The principle is still the same: The Holy Spirit renews and blesses churches with new seasons of growth through the passions and dreams of laypeople.

Here's an example. Early in my (David's) ministry career, I started a neighborhood-based small-group ministry in a downtown church that had thirty-seven parking spaces for five hundred people. People literally came from all four directions, within about ten miles, to attend. After a number of years, I was called to pastor another church. Six years later, that first church asked me to come and re-launch their small-group ministry. They'd undergone a lot of change in a few years. The young "drive-in" families had grown older; they now had teenage kids who wanted to connect with their peers, so those families had largely left this commuter church to join congregations closer to where they lived. The senior pastor had changed, and the church on the whole had lost a lot of key people. Membership had declined to around two hundred fifty. The small-group ministry needed to be redefined.

Jessica lived near the church. She had married since I'd been there, but she continued to have a heart for all the latchkey kids in the neighborhood. The church had always had a child enrichment center, but Jessica also started a "Mom's Day Out" small group, which had grown from one group to a ministry that reached one hundred moms. God had grown what was blooming in Jessica's heart and lifted up this moms' ministry as the new season and new generation that would define where the church needed to go. The dream started with one woman and grew to become the focused direction of the entire church. Building on that moms' ministry, the church built bridges to their husbands as well. Entire families were becoming members. It started with one seedling in Jessica's heart and grew to renew an entire congregation.

Never underestimate the power of what God can grow out of the tiny seeds He plants in hearts.

Jesus went through all the towns and villages, teaching in their synagogues, preaching the good news of the kingdom and healing every disease and sickness. When he saw the crowds, he had compassion on them, because they were harassed and helpless, like sheep without a shepherd. Then he said to his disciples, "The harvest is plentiful but the workers are few. Ask the Lord of the harvest, therefore, to send out workers into his harvest field" (Matthew 9:35–38).

What needs harvesting in your church? in your small-group ministry? in you?

Summary Questions

1. What gifts, passions, and/or natural talents do you see in yourself and those around you that need to be freed to serve in small-group ministry?

2. What will be the greatest challenges for your church in this empowerment process?

3. How do the design questions for developing small groups foster creative thinking about small groups?

4. Make two columns, one entitled "Fears" and the other entitled "Freedoms." As you reflect on this chapter, list the fears and freedoms that happen when small groups are developed by growing what's blooming. Which column is longer? What does this tell you?

CHAPTER SEVEN:

NURTURE WHAT'S GROWING

Brian loved being part of a small group, having had a positive experience with it in college, so when he and Jen got married and moved to a new city, he was delighted that they found a spiritually alive church with a vibrant small-group ministry. There they joined a group of young couples, who soon became good friends while studying together what it means to have a Christian marriage. It was a solid foundation for Brian and Jen's new life together as husband and wife.

After two years, though, Brian became restless. He longed for more depth and wanted the group to build spiritual accountability into their relationships with one another. Most of the couples had other ideas—they wanted to keep studying marriage principles. Jen loved the people in their group and just wanted to stay with their friends, no matter what agenda they chose.

With a great deal of patience and prayer, Brian and Jen worked through their differences. Brian deferred to his wife's desires and stayed with the group, but he also became part of an accountability group with three other men. They met for breakfast several times a month and began the process of developing spiritual disciplines and accountability. What started as a potential conflict turned out to be a win/win situation for Brian and Jen. Together they enjoyed the support and friendship of couples like themselves, and Brian also found additional spiritual depth in his men's accountability group. At the end of the next season, they prayerfully made the decision to leave the couples group and form a study/accountability group that involved a deeper level of sharing. Together they became aware of God's special timing and how He provided the next step for them.

Brian was alert to how important it is to nurture what's growing. God doesn't grow us to a certain point and then abandon us; He provides opportunity to nurture the growth He gives, and in the process, we develop spiritual depth. Part of nurturing what's growing includes an awareness of three "rules" or realities that are true of all small groups:

(1) *All groups have multiple agendas.*

(2) *All groups have life cycles.*

(3) *All groups need to build relationships.*

All Groups Have Multiple Agendas

We began to discuss agendas in chapter 6; recall that except for those rare "hybrid" groups that have multiple agendas in equal proportion, small groups have a primary agenda and then secondary agendas. People are too complex—and too precious—to so neatly compartmentalize their lives that they have only one agenda for their small groups. Relationship-building ("being") groups inevitably support and care for one another. Even the most task-oriented ("working") groups build relationships too. There's a learning component that comes almost by default from growing together in a small group. Nurturing the various agendas enriches the life of the group.

Brian and Jen experienced multiple agendas in the group for young couples—they built relationships with one another, cared for one another, and learned about marriage together. One of the reasons they continued to enjoy the group was that they were wise enough to change the agenda as the group changed. They nurtured what was growing, and in their case, it was their families! As these young marrieds became pregnant, they changed the learning focus of their agenda from marriage to parenting. By the third season, Brian and Jen sensed God leading them to another agenda completely—a learning agenda—as well as to another small group. The couples group they were a part of continued to meet as well. As people's needs change, both spiritually and personally, their small group agendas and the small groups themselves will also change.

The Coffee Break groups in one small rural church are focused on learning through Bible study, but the people in them are also changed by the relationship-building and caring for one another that are integral to its ministry. Karen is a member of that church and has attended Coffee Break since it began five years ago. Her family had no church background and no interest in the church, but week after week Karen's small group prayed for them faithfully. Over time Karen's mom saw a change in her daughter and became curious to know what made her the softer, warmer woman she was becoming.

She eventually responded to Karen's invitation to attend Coffee Break; afterward, she cried all the way home, overwhelmed by how kind everyone had been to her. She was extremely overweight and had grown used to being rejected and belittled, but Coffee Break was different: There she was drawn in and accepted for who she was. She stayed with the group because they continued to warmly welcome and nurture her. As she fed on the Word, she also began attending the church with her husband. After a time, she was baptized, and she and her husband became members.

The nurturing continued as God used the power of His love and of Karen's mom's testimony, along with the prayers of her small group, to draw in Karen's sister and her daughter as well. Then Karen's sister became convicted that she shouldn't be living with her boyfriend and moved out. She too became a believer. Eventually even Karen's grandmother committed her life to Christ. Now everyone is praying for the boyfriend of Karen's sister. He also has begun attending the little church that cares. The multiple agendas of one small group worked together to nurture what was growing, and God used it all to draw an entire family into a relationship with Christ and His church.

All Groups Have Life Cycles

The second reality of small groups is that they all have life cycles. We often celebrate their beginnings, but somehow we have received the mistaken message that ending a group is a bad thing. It's not! Small groups are living, growing organisms that have a start and a finish. Small-group life cycles will also vary, just as there are distinct differences in the life cycles of plants.

The purpose of the group determines the length of its life cycle; the purpose will also determine which of the small-group principles it will include in its life cycle(s). Sometimes the purpose changes and the group continues, and sometimes the group ends when its original purpose is accomplished. Again, that's good!

For example, short-term task groups will have a different understanding of support-and-belonging principles than a Twelve-Step recovery group. A spiritual disciplines group will understand the principles of risk-taking and decision-making differently than a dinner-for-eight group. The more in-depth the purpose, and the more agendas the group includes (being, working, caring, learning), the more likely the group will be to incorporate all the sociological principles.

No matter what kind of small group it is, however, it has its own life cycle(s). As previously mentioned, this understanding relieves a lot of guilt for leaders who believe they've failed when their groups end. Part of nurturing a group is helping everyone—especially the leader—see that small groups have both a beginning and an end, and, therefore, helping a specific group to end well when its purpose has been accomplished.

This realization was a huge relief for Danell and Ken. They initially started a small group with three other Christian couples in order to network and be connected. The group clicked, and they looked forward to spending time studying the Bible together. Over several months' time they deepened in their knowledge of the Word, one another, and their commitment to growing in their Christian walk.

But then "life" interfered. First one couple couldn't meet at their agreed-upon time, and then another had a scheduling conflict. Because they loved having everyone together, the group didn't want to meet unless everyone could attend, and gradually they stopped meeting entirely. Because they'd never discussed their specific purpose, Danell felt like a failure when the group fizzled and died. However, when she grasped the concepts of life cycles and agendas, the lights went on.

"I finally understood what happened," she said. "Our unwritten agendas had been accomplished. Out of the four couples, two of the women had joined me in Coffee Break leadership, and all four guys golfed together." They'd achieved the desired networking and connecting with other Christian couples, and now those needs were being nurtured in other kinds of small groups. "If I had been more aware," she went on, "we could have come to a new 'covenant' and decided to move into [the principles of] transformation and accountability, but being aware of the life cycles of small groups relieved me of the burden of guilt for letting our couples Bible study end."

Nurturing can come in different ways when we see that small groups have life cycles. Sometimes it's a person's (or couple's) participation in a particular group that has a life cycle. Randy and Lee had led their couples group for several years and were feeling restless. They weren't sure if they were supposed to leave the group, but they definitely had some new ideas about starting and leading a different one. They were facing a crossroads in determining whether their group—or at least their leadership in it—was coming to a close.

Though they were privately frustrated, they only discussed their concerns with their small-group coach. Eventually they decided to continue with their group for another season. Several factors led them to that decision, including that there didn't seem to be a good way to replace their leadership, and some relationships within the group needed their support. As it turned out, there *were* significant needs that required their unique leadership as well as the support of the group's relationships. Looking back, Randy and Lee could see God's hand in leading them to stay for one more season; after that, several signs indicated that this would be a good time in the life of the group for them to leave and hand over the leadership to others.

It takes consistent prayer and discernment to know the correct timing for significant changes, but by paying attention to group dynamics as they work together in tension or harmony, we get clues. No single incident or feeling is probably enough to make a change, but it may be the first step in a process that will lead to significant change when the time is right. God knew that Randy and Lee's gifts were needed to nurture their small group in the final season of their leadership in it. God also made clear when that season was over by providing the right leaders to take their place. In this way, God also made it plain that the life cycle of the small group was *not* over. Growing people—and nurturing them through that growth—is God's work, and He will guide the life cycles of groups and leaders in His timing.

All Groups Need to Build Relationships

The third reality of all small groups is that they need to build relationships: They aren't lifeless or static but are living, breathing organisms. Building relationships is integral because small groups are made up of individuals who think and feel and laugh and cry and work and play, individuals who need to be a part of something bigger than themselves. Building those relationships is a process, starting with a getting-acquainted phase, then forming friendships, then risking vulnerability, and finally achieving community. Sometimes that initial getting-acquainted stage, as simple as it seems, is the hardest part.

GETTING ACQUAINTED

Getting acquainted is the foundation of relationships. During this stage people give factual information about what they feel safe in sharing, such as relating historical knowledge, discussing public events, and telling what they *think*. Even when people join their groups voluntarily, leaders will need to be intentional in helping them get to know one another. They often long to be connected but avoid connecting; they crave community but run from it; they long to get acquainted but don't know how.

Peggy led a small-group Bible study for almost a year before she tackled the importance of simply getting acquainted. It wasn't that the group didn't like each other or talk to one another, but that they were too nice—maddeningly so! They politely shared their insights on the passages they were studying, and they always did what was proper. The atmosphere was sterile, and everyone stayed safely "in their heads," never sharing their hearts and lives with one another.

Peggy was incredibly frustrated. Finally, in desperation, she scrapped the night's lesson and spent the whole hour doing icebreakers with the group. They revealed their favorite foods, where they grew up, how they met as couples, where they would most like to spend a two-week vacation, and so on. They even dared to share their pet peeves and their most embarrassing moment. They laughed together and told stories, giving more of themselves and their lives in that one hour than they had in all their months of Bible study. It allowed them to get to know one another in a relational way; in fact, that one week of icebreakers revolutionized the group, setting the stage for much more authentic, life-application Bible study in the weeks ahead.

Part of nurturing what's growing means recognizing what a group or an individual needs and then providing for that need, even if it means starting over. In our small groups, we will encounter people like those in Peggy's group, and we will need to nurture them. Our challenge is to get through that getting-acquainted stage so that we can hear the cries they won't utter, heal the wounds they won't acknowledge, and lead them to the Savior they might either take for granted or think they don't need.

FORMING FRIENDSHIPS

After people get acquainted in a small group, they're ready to form friendships. During this stage of relationship-building, people become comfortable sharing things happening at the present time, and they affirm what they enjoy about one another. They move beyond what they *think* to communicate how they *feel*. It's at this stage that people feel accepted and know they belong. This is the stage for leaders to nurture their groups by providing opportunity for them to hang out together and to create a safe place for people to talk about life in greater depth. They begin to communicate their hopes and dreams and fears. Leaders who personally extend the gift of friendship make it possible for others to become friends as well.

Sam tells this delightful story about her learning that building relationships is important—even when you're already friends with everyone in your group.

Once I was leading a Bible study in my neighborhood. About eight of us had met the year before, so we all knew each other very well. This was the first meeting of the new fall season. Many women had invited friends. For this first meeting we now had sixteen women, half of whom did not know anyone and had never done Bible study before. I was really nervous because although I had attended the Bible study the year before, I had never led the group. It was a little intimidating leading a Bible study with women who know almost everything about you: when you get behind on mowing your lawn or taking out the trash and what you look like on your worst days.

The women came, stood around with their friends and drank coffee. I knew we were on a tight schedule because of childcare time commitments, so I instructed everyone to sit down and get their Bibles and lessons out. I opened with prayer and we got started. It was going miserably. I would ask a question—silence—maybe one person would answer. There was no fun exchange of ideas. After plugging our way through a couple of questions, it dawned on me that most of these people didn't even know each other's names. So I apologized, explained I was really nervous, and asked if we could start over with some introductions. We all laughed, then went around the room asking names and what their favorite breakfast cereal was. We found out who liked healthy oatmeal, who was on a diet, and who was really honest by admitting they ate Captain Crunch.

The ice was broken, people heard themselves talk and knew some silly things about each other. Then I restarted the lesson. Now it went great. I've learned how important building relationships is. I've also learned that this is essential at the beginning but there might be days after you've met for a while when people are feeling isolated and you need to again focus on building relationships. On those days I focus less on getting the lesson done and let the group sidetrack on issues about life.

Sam's small-group Bible study was already filled with close friendships, but when her friends added a few more friends, they needed to build relationships gradually. Only then were they ready and willing to share more vulnerably with one another.

RISKING VULNERABILITY

For many people, it's only within the safety of mutual friendship that they will risk vulnerability. When a small group moves to this stage of building relationships, members let you peek inside their hearts, exposing their weaknesses and struggles as well as their hopes and dreams. Trust is foundational for getting to this point. Part of the leader's role is to keep his or her fingers on the pulse of both the group and its members in order to provide the nurture needed for an atmosphere of trust. The leader also needs to personally model vulnerability as a signal that this is a safe place to bare your soul.

Bill and Gloria deliberately chose to join a small group with a rather superficial agenda because they didn't want to risk vulnerability. The only goal for the empty-nester couples was to enjoy being together at this stage of their lives. They had dinner in one another's homes, played games or watched videos, and enjoyed lively conversation, content to keep their relationships at a friendship level.

The truth is, Bill and Gloria were carefully guarding a deep secret and didn't want it exposed. But the couple leading the group knew how to nurture, and they picked up signs of stress in Bill and Gloria's relationship. Sometimes Gloria came alone, apologizing for Bill and making excuses for his absence. At those times she seemed distraught and distracted. Something wasn't quite right.

The leaders believed it was their responsibility to care for their members and decided to express their concerns. Rather than doing so with the whole group, however, the wife of the leadership duo invited Gloria out for coffee. She was gentle in her approach, expressing love and concern for both Bill and Gloria, opening doors by creating a safe place for Gloria to share whatever she chose.

Gloria saw the lifeline being tossed to her, and she took it. With wracking sobs she poured out the whole story. Just a couple of years earlier, Bill had been the victim of a hostile corporate takeover and had been released from a high-paying job. His self-esteem and even his identity as a man were drastically compromised. Just at that time, someone in his golf league introduced Bill to the mind-numbing pleasure of illegal drugs. He became addicted to cocaine; while Gloria frantically tried to hold their lives together, he slipped further into the dark world of substance abuse. She saw their life savings slowly draining away, and she was desperately attempting to protect both her family's reputation and whatever assets they had left. They were both filled with guilt and shame. She felt completely alone and helpless.

The loving nurture of her leaders gave Gloria hope. At first she was too ashamed to share what was happening with the entire group, but as she continued to build trust, she eventually shared her struggle with all of them. They also reached out and embraced her, praying faithfully for Bill and Gloria. Unfortunately, Bill simply could not master the demons that plagued him and continued to spiral downward. After several years he died of a heart attack complicated by drug abuse. The small group that originally was meant only to build superficial relationships provided the love, loyalty, and prayer support that Gloria needed to weather this storm and begin a new life.

The whole group benefited from this depth of relationship. Sometimes the church can be a place of well-kept secrets and lonely pain; this group provided the appropriate place for honesty, love, and healing. Everyone in the body of Christ became a minister of God's mercy as they moved to that final stage of building relationships—achieving community.

ACHIEVING COMMUNITY

Small groups at this stage share unique relational depth—emotionally, interpersonally, and spiritually. These groups love one another deeply, carry one another's burdens, and admonish one another. They affirm what they appreciate about one another, express affection toward one another, and are honest in confronting issues (good and bad) in the group.

A small group of five leadership couples in Calvary Church have enjoyed this kind of authentic community for fourteen years. Each person is involved in at least one other leadership role in the church, but it's in this small group that they're nurtured and replenished for the ministry they do. They share life together. They pray for one another, go camping together, eat out together, and support one another emotionally and spiritually. They have comforted other members in the death of a child and rejoiced at the birth of a new baby. They laugh and cry together. They stretch each other mentally and spiritually. They speak truth to one another, but they do it with great love.

Not every group will attain all these stages of relationship-building. Not all of them should! The level of relationship depth will be determined by the group's type and the group's agenda. A short-term working group gathered around a specific project will likely never attain the depth that a grief support group will. Achieving community requires a level of intimacy that takes time, which not every group will have. Short-term groups in the early stages of their life cycle will not go as deep as "older" groups. That's fine—the short-term group may be at exactly the right place. We need to have realistic expectations in order to endure and persevere in ministry. Nurture can come at a variety of levels.

In fact, one of the challenges for leaders is to be responsible to the whole group when the members are at different stages of their willingness to be vulnerable. We're not all wired the same way. Some people's lives are an open book; others open the door of their lives very cautiously before letting anyone inside.

Leslie led this kind of mixed-bag group. One of the members, Candice, was a swing-the-door-wide-open person—in a matter of minutes, you knew how Candice was feeling that day. Whether with the group or in the grocery store, she did not hesitate to tell you exactly what was happening between her and her husband, Danny (fights, sex, money problems, you name it). Leslie and her Bible study group heard it all, much to the dismay of Dorothy.

Dorothy was a person who only cautiously let people peek inside the door of her life. Leslie perceived that on the whole, the group's anxiety was increasing in proportion to the openness of Candice, so for the common good, she tried to limit Candice's sharing. She began by avoiding eye contact with her, which sometimes worked. Eventually she had to phone Candice and explain that some people didn't feel comfortable with all the details of her personal relationships; could she limit her sharing to a few minutes, please?

Leslie and her co-leader also tried to give Candice talk times outside of Bible study, where she could share more. Since she was such an open person, Candice didn't take much offense at their trying to help her set boundaries. All these efforts didn't completely fix the problem, but they were an important part of the leader's role to responsibly nurture everyone in the group at a level where she was comfortable.

Four Goals, Four Diagnostic Questions

We nurture what's growing (1) to enhance the spiritual development of each group member, (2) to determine the health and depth of the group as a whole, (3) to train members for leadership by identifying and mobilizing their gifts and talents, and (4) to contribute to the growth of the entire small-group ministry. We accomplish these goals through a series of diagnostic questions that help give a vision of how to keep groups vital as they're together over a period of time:

(1) *How is the leader doing?*
(2) *How is each individual member doing?*
(3) *What's happening in/around the group?*
(4) *What principle(s) is the group working on?*

Asking these diagnostic questions doesn't necessarily mean a group will change—it may continue in a new season with the previous agenda. But leaders and coaches/managers need to get in the habit of addressing these questions a minimum of once—preferably twice—annually. Doing so as a group encourages everyone to answer the question, "What's our next move?" Because a small group is a dynamic organism, not everyone may like the upcoming season. Some will leave; they need the freedom to do so without feeling guilt or failure, either as members or as leaders.

HOW IS THE LEADER DOING?

The first diagnostic question that must be answered in order to nurture the life of a small group focuses on the leader: How is he or she doing? Often the group's health will not exceed the health of its leader. The leader needs to be nurtured in order to nurture others—no one is an island doing his or her own thing. Organisms are part of a body, and each leader needs to be accountable to someone to ensure the health of the entire group.

At the same time, because leaders are leaders, they take responsibility for their own health. They don't wait for someone to *tell* them they need a checkup—they take their own temperature, check their own pulse, and ask for help when they need it. They ask questions like these: Where am I in my discipleship journey? What season of life am I in? What problems might the managers or others help me address? What gifts, talents, and passions are surfacing in me? Leaders begin with self-reflection, which informs the nurturing they receive from those to whom they are accountable.

Sometimes the questions for self-reflection need to be adapted to fit a particular situation. Brenda had expertly led a Bible study group for a number of years. But after her husband walked out and married his much-younger former administrative assistant, leaving Brenda alone with two kids to support, she developed a new passion—reaching other single moms, starting a support group for them. When she shared her dream with her small-group manager, however, she realized she needed to do some serious self-reflection before she'd be ready to lead the group she desired. Her manager asked questions specific to Brenda's situation: What motivated her to lead this kind of group? What gifts would she bring as a leader? How would they benefit the group? Where was she in her own healing process? Was she ready to lead the kind of group she was proposing?

In the end, Brenda realized that she had too many unresolved anger issues to be helpful to others struggling with a similar situation. She ended up joining a support group and working through her own issues first. Then she was able to walk others through a similar challenge.

How Is Each Individual Member Doing?

The questions that the small-group manager/coach will ask a leader are the same questions that a leader must ask regarding each member. Does this person have a special need for care and support at this time? Where is this person in his/her life circumstances? Where is this person in his/her faith journey and development as a disciple? What is going on around this person? What are some of the gifts, talents, and passions I see in this person?

Bill and Gloria's small-group leaders asked these questions before they approached Gloria out of concern for what they saw happening in her and Bill's lives. Because Gloria sensed their genuine concern, she felt safe in sharing her husband's addiction and the chaos it was causing in their lives. Loving nurture starts with caring about the people we're growing, not what's happening with the structure of the ministry. Growing people includes annual or semiannual checkups to make sure the leaders and members are healthy and feeling cared for.

Of course, that doesn't mean everyone will be *happy*! Leaders and managers are not miracle workers, and small groups are not a magic pill that automatically makes contented people. We will never be able to meet everyone's needs, and we shouldn't try to; boundary setting is essential for the leader's health. These diagnostic questions are "preventive medicine," helping leaders and coaches/managers keep their focus on growing people responsibly and also becoming aware of issues that need to be addressed.

WHAT'S HAPPENING IN/AROUND THE GROUP?

The small group itself is an organism that needs to be nurtured in order to grow; leaders are concerned not only with nurturing individual members but also with nurturing the entire group. How is the group as a whole doing? What season are they in? What's in their future? How are they likely to grow?

When leaders nurture the growth of a small group, they discover several likely outcomes. Nurturing the members and being nurtured as leaders will prepare the way for determining how to nurture the group of which both leader and members are a part. The group may decide to stick with the same agenda for the next season. Everyone may remain with the group. Some members may choose to leave. The group may change and plan a new agenda the next season. Or it may simply want a new challenge within the same agenda. A member may leave to lead a new group or for other leadership. Sometimes the group becomes sponsors or advocates of another group. It may divide into two groups. Maybe the leader will leave or all the members will become leaders. The group may end.

None of these outcomes is necessarily right or wrong, good or bad. The beauty of nurturing both individuals and groups is that God uses our growing maturity to create fresh avenues for ministry.

A men's volleyball team chose the option of changing its agenda. For a number of years they'd met on Thursday nights just to hit the ball around and build relationships. It was a great entry-level small group, but the passion of their two leaders was short-term/long-term missions, and their passion was contagious.

The group decided to go on a short-term outreach to Arkansas, which was the beginning of a major shift in their agenda. They continued to add a mission component to what they did and eventually became the hub of their men's rural mission group. They redefined themselves from just a volleyball team to a volleyball team that also is a mission to the world. It happened because they sat down and asked, "What season are we in? What are we all about? What's our growth edge?"

A couples' ministry likewise got to the point where they knew they needed to focus their energy outward as well as inward. One group chose to sponsor a child from a developing nation. Several others became involved in a program called "Families Moving Forward," a ministry to the homeless in their community. One week every quarter their church opens its doors to the homeless to live in the church for one week. These groups sign up together to serve those staying in the church at that time; they prepare meals, clean the building, and form relationships. Those who have become involved say they receive far more than they give through the experience. It has been a faith-building and stretching experience for those who have participated.

No matter what option a group chooses as the next season in its growth cycle, eventually the group will either redefine itself or end. No group meets *solely* for its own sake. People don't sign up for community for community's sake *alone*. The purpose of building community is to serve one another or go out into the world and serve. Part of nurturing is knowing when closure is the next step.

What Principle(s) Is the Group Working On?

One way to determine where a small group is in its life cycle is to look at which sociological principle(s) is/are the focus. Where are we in our development? Have we moved beyond support and belonging? What must we strive to attain? What's our growth edge?

Once again, it's true that not all small groups will address every small-group principle. But using the principles as a guide to evaluate the growth of a group is extremely helpful. Identifying the principle(s) at work in a group can narrow the focus on what needs to be nurtured.

The couples groups that served the homeless had a wise leader nudging them beyond simply claiming Jesus as Savior and Lord to becoming His servants. They moved beyond the principles of support and belonging to accountability and risk-taking. The volleyball-team-turned-missions-center did the same. They became leaders that motivated others to serve.

Nurturing what's growing honors where God is at work in people's lives. Leaders have the awesome privilege of watering—with our love, support, and leadership—all that God is cultivating and blessing. We till the soil so that the nutrients of His grace sink deep into the roots, and we rejoice at the growth He gives. On the journey of drawing people closer to God, we hold loosely to our responsibility as leaders and hold tightly to Him and all He intends the group members to be and do with His help.

Summary Questions

1. What needs nurturing in the small groups you lead or are a part of?

2. What level of relationship-building do you see in your small groups? What needs to be challenged or changed? What needs to be celebrated?

3. Is there diversity in the agendas of your small groups? Which agenda dominates, if any?

4. Where are your small groups in the life-cycle process? How do you celebrate the groups whose agendas have been completed? How do you urge forward those who seem to be stuck?

5. Have you evaluated your small groups regularly? What systems do you need to put into place to ensure that consistent evaluation occurs?

CHAPTER EIGHT:

TRANSPLANT WHAT NEEDS ROOM TO GROW

I (Betty) poured another cup of coffee for the four guests seated around my dining room table and smiled at their eager faces. "You're probably all wondering why I invited you here this morning," I said.

They glanced at one another and laughed. "Yes, as a matter of fact, we are," one of the women confessed.

"Well," I said, "I have a vision, and I can't wait to share it."

During the next half hour, I shared my dream for each of them to take what they'd learned in our Bible study and begin a program in their own church. All four women were from the same congregation and had faithfully attended my church's Coffee Break for a number of years. Two of them had been in the group I led. They were warm, wonderful women who loved people and loved God. They had obvious leadership gifts. The roots of their faith were deep into the Word.

They were ready for more than just attending our study; they were ready to be transplanted and begin their own. Ours had grown in size and, frankly, we'd become a little too comfortable and complacent about reaching out to new people. A little pruning would probably be just the stimulus we needed. We had to transplant what needed room to grow, and what needed room to grow was our Coffee Break and this little core of women from another church across town.

God had prepared them—and me—for this moment. They caught the vision immediately. Ideas and enthusiasm bounced off the walls as this excited little group began to make plans. Almost intuitively they saw how their gifts would fit together. Linda would coordinate the nursery and Story Hour program for preschoolers. Sally would use her administrative gifts to coordinate the Coffee Break. Mary's shepherding gifts were a natural fit for leading a group. Cora would provide help wherever it was most needed. Together this energized foursome resolved to meet again, and as our time together ended, they expressed deep appreciation for receiving the gift of beginning another Bible study. Mary spoke for all of them: "I have loved attending Coffee Break, but I was ready for a new challenge. I'm not sure I would have returned next year. This is exactly what I needed to keep going." And to keep growing.

In transplanting what needed room to grow, two small-group Bible study ministries thrived instead of one. Our Coffee Break had space to welcome more people, and the freshly brewed Coffee Break across town attracted a whole different group of women—they also grew. People, like plants, need room to grow. Sometimes being transplanted is exactly what God has in mind for making this happen.

In reflecting on that satisfying interaction in my dining room, I recalled the first time I bought two beautiful hanging baskets to decorate the front porch of my home. Geraniums, ageratum, alyssum, and Vinca vine combined in a riot of color and lush fullness. I looked forward to enjoying their beauty all summer . . . but it didn't happen. When I purchased them, the plants were already so thick in the baskets that there was no room for them to grow. I wasn't wise enough to prune them, and as the summer wore on, they became more and more scraggly, drooping over the basket sides in exhaustion from vying for whatever space they could find to expand their roots and blossoms. If only I'd thinned them out. If only I'd put them in a bigger pot. If only I'd divided them in half. If only. If only. But I didn't. They couldn't thrive, and I didn't enjoy them.

Like my hanging baskets, small groups need long-term care in order to thrive. This includes transplanting what needs room to grow. In fact, it's in this stage that the organic nature of small groups is especially evident.

In a greenhouse nursery, all the plants have the same requirements in common: they all need water, soil, and nutrients. However, the proportion of water, kind of soil and nutrients, and the atmosphere that each requires will vary; as a result, the plants will differ—their life stages will be different, and the kinds of care they need will be different. The nursery worker respects each plant and tailors its care so that it can be all it was intended to be. Some plants find room to grow by being thinned out. Sometimes the gardener takes a cutting from an existing plant and grows another just like it. Sometimes one plant is grafted onto another, and a whole new plant form develops. The attendant may find a plant has burst and needs to be divided and put in different parts of the garden. Sometimes plants die, and the seeds are saved for replanting.

Small groups, like plants, need to be dealt with uniquely. Small-group leaders and managers are like gardeners, and part of their role is to help members—and the group itself—thrive by being attentive to what needs room to grow. Our Creator God has the perfect plan for each of His one-of-a-kind creations, and as cultivators, small-group leaders carry out His work.

Transplanting what needs room to grow happens on several levels. Sometimes leaders need to be transplanted in order to have room to grow. At times individual members do. A whole group may need to be transplanted into a new agenda. Or an entire part of the small-group ministry may need to be transplanted in order for the ministry to have room to grow. Regardless—always, always—those in leadership stay focused on what God is doing and then follow His leading. This is what keeps small groups and their members expanding and dynamic. God blesses those who are attentive to what needs room to grow.

The story in Acts 6 is a good example. The young New Testament church faced a growth crisis and a capacity problem: The number of Jesus' disciples was growing daily, but the leadership was staying the same. The apostles were doing everything, including teaching, prayer, and oversight of the daily distribution of food for the widows. In the crunch, some of the widows were being neglected, and their families complained. The growth of the church was limited to the capacity of the apostles, and they were maxed out.

At that point, the Twelve gathered all the disciples together to talk about the problem, challenging them to "choose seven men . . . who [were] known to be full of the Spirit and wisdom" (v. 3). These seven could then be responsible for seeing to the daily needs of the widows, while the apostles gave their "attention to prayer and the ministry of the word" (v. 4). The results were astounding: "The word of God spread. The number of disciples in Jerusalem increased rapidly, and a large number of priests became obedient to the faith" (v. 7).

The Transplanting Process

God didn't intend for the apostles to do everything in the church. He gifted and called them to a very specific task—prayer and preaching. He blessed them when they identified, trained, and empowered others to use the gifts He had given them.

God doesn't mean for any of us to do everything either. That's why He made us a body whose parts need each other, and why He gifts people in different ways. We learn an important process from the apostles' experience, one that also applies to small-group growth. First, the apostles clarified and defined the need so they had specific information about the nature of the problem. Second, they clearly defined their own roles. In their case, they became acutely focused, narrowing their leadership responsibilities to praying and teaching the Word of God. Third, they identified the gifts of others, equipped them—laid hands on them—and released them to serve.

DEFINE THE PROBLEM AND CLARIFY THE NEED

When we follow these steps and transplant what needs room to grow, we experience God's applause. We begin by doing what the apostles did: figure out what the problem is. The statement "A problem well defined is a problem half solved" really is true. In the apostles' situation and in small-group ministry, what looks like a crisis can instead be an opportunity, if only we're able to define the problem and see the possibilities for something positive. Crisis gives us a chance to self-define more and more so we can empower people in just the right place, the right way, and the right time that God designs.

Sometimes a problem first becomes evident when a spirit of restlessness or discontent surfaces. That's how an emerging crisis surfaced in the Moms' Morning ministry at my (David's) church. We had a successful ministry to moms of young children, having grown to almost two hundred women in small groups over a number of years. One day a couple of the leaders came to me and said that some of the women were unhappy because the groups were no longer relevant to their lives. I invited those who were interested to join me in discussing the future of the Moms' Morning ministry in order to define the issues and be clear about what they needed. About ninety showed up; I broke them into small groups and asked them to define where they were when they started Moms' Morning, where they were today, and how the two were different.

All the women affirmed the important role the groups had played in their lives, but many of them no longer had preschoolers and toddlers, and the content of the groups didn't fit them anymore. Their season of life had changed, and they wanted to be part of a group that was more relevant to their life stage. They wanted groups for parenting elementary-school kids and for parenting teenagers. They also wanted their faith stretched and challenged. As they shared their needs, I realized that we needed not just one expression of Moms' Morning, but three—moms of toddlers/preschoolers, of elementary-age children, and of teenagers.

BE CLEAR ABOUT THE LEADER'S ROLE

I also knew that we couldn't ask our current Moms' Morning ministry leaders to add one more thing to their small-group plate. I could feel their stress level rise in anticipation of the very thought! They were focused on what they were passionate about and wanted to continue in those roles. I freed them to continue to do what God was blessing, and I trusted that if He was leading us to grow in this way, He would also provide the leadership.

Leaders need to stay focused on what they do well. They need to know what their spiritual gifts are, what they're passionate about, and what they value. They need to understand how they're wired according to their personality. They need to concentrate on the unique kingdom contribution that God has asked them to make. Jim Collins, in his book *Good to Great,* says that companies go from good to great when their people focus on what they do well and empower others to do the same. He calls it the "hedgehog principle." Hedgehogs do one thing, and they do it really well: they know how to roll up into a ball and protect themselves. Collins believes that the more specific and focused leaders are, the more successful they'll be. In interviews with executive leadership, Collins found that good executives get about 50 percent right on a "talent" test, but great executives get 90 percent right. In biblical language, they know what they're called to and gifted for, and they know what they're not called to and not gifted for. Like the hedgehog and like the apostles in Acts 6, they don't try to do everything.

Train, Empower, and Release Others

Again, I couldn't ask our Mom's Morning leaders to do everything, so I divided the ministry into the three kinds of groups we'd identified and asked if any of the women expressing a need for change would be willing to consider leading the two new groups we'd named. Several volunteered, some eagerly and some with hesitation. But leadership is more than just volunteering. These women also agreed to go through training and a discernment process, and they agreed to be part of a leadership team. Our commitment was to train them, equip them, pray for them, and stand beside them. Then, like the newly appointed deacons in Acts 6, once these new leaders were equipped and were part of a support system, they were released to serve.

RESULTS: GOD'S BLESSING

It was a scary move for our church. We had a thriving Mom's Morning ministry, and we'd just lopped off two-thirds of it. We had history here. Letting go of what was comfortable and familiar to embrace an uncertain future at times seemed downright irresponsible. Many leaders expressed their apprehension also: "Dave, if you divide us into three pieces, not only could the pieces not work, but we will probably kill the Mother Goose in the beginning of it too." I understood their anxiety.

Our Mom's Morning ministry did suffer initially. It dropped from nearly two hundred to about one hundred twenty. Within a year, however, not only had the original group grown back to its original size, but the two new groups were averaging between fifty and one hundred women as well. Instead of one kind of group reaching around two hundred women, we had three kinds of groups reaching around three hundred fifty. Sometimes we'll be challenged to walk by faith and not by sight when we transplant what we believe needs room to grow. God blessed our obedience and our step of faith.

Transplanting for Growth

Transplanting happens in a variety of ways, and the previous story illustrates just one—members leaving to lead a new group (or, in this case, multiple groups). Other ways to transplant what needs room to grow include some members leaving the group; setting a new agenda for the next season; having members leave for other leadership; replacing the leader; all members becoming leaders; and ending the group. You may know of others. We'll share a few stories of groups that have faced the challenge of transplanting what needed room to grow.

ENDING THE GROUP

Sometimes the best way for growth to happen is for a group to end. Sounds strange, but it's true. Remember the "rule" for small groups that says all of them have life cycles? This is one way the rule not only translates into reality but also promotes growth. Small groups are not designed to go on and on and on—they're designed with a specific agenda in mind, and when that agenda is accomplished, the group ends.

Several years ago five couples from the same church, all struggling with infertility, formed a support group to encourage one another. They met on Sunday afternoons and together worked through all the issues that accompany the challenge of infertility. They explored their feelings of anger toward God for not answering their prayers for a child, and after a period of time they got to the point where they believed He still loved them and had a plan for them, even though they had not given birth.

Then an amazing thing happened. One by one, each of the women in the group became pregnant. First, one was pregnant and four were not. Then two were pregnant and three were not. Three were pregnant and two were not; four were pregnant and one was not; and finally, all five were pregnant. Because these five couples had bonded together and bared their souls to one another, they stuck together through what at the beginning of the pregnancies was a very difficult time. Because they'd worked through their anger and sorrow and grasped who they were in Christ—with or without children—no one abandoned the group because some were with child and others weren't.

They were committed to one another. However, the purpose of the group was to share support for infertility. That purpose no longer existed once they all became parents, so they celebrated what God had blessed and ended the group. Though a special bond remains whenever they see one another, these couples have moved on to other arenas of service.

SOME MEMBERS LEAVING THE GROUP

Another way to find room to grow is when some group members choose not to return for the next season. This is common. It doesn't necessarily mean the group has gone bad or that anything is wrong—it illustrates again that because small groups are organic, different people will be at different stages in their spiritual life cycles and will have different needs. When leaders acknowledge and respect those differences, everyone in the group is freed from the burden of false guilt for "abandoning" the others if a person or couple decides to leave.

Sometimes, of course, a leader's role may be to encourage a person to stay if he or she believes the person is leaving for the wrong reasons. But the leader is *not* responsible for controlling who stays in the group or who leaves; he or she is charged with providing an atmosphere for growth. Then we leave the results to God.

My (David's) church's fathering team faced the situation of having members leave the group when several of the eight guys wanted to meet at a different time. They were still excited about our agenda, but our meeting time didn't work into their schedules, so they dropped out. That gave those of us remaining an opportunity to move into a new season of growth. We republicized our small group and were able to add new guys in a new season.

Some Members Leaving to Lead a New Group

In fact, the four guys who left our fathering team then formed a new team. It was the same kind of group, only in a different setting and at a different time. The two groups were able to share the same game plans and chalk-talks because different guys met in each group. And each group was able to grow because a few key leaders were transplanted into a new setting.

It's not all bad when members leave. Without moving forward or changing in some way, some small groups get stuck in "holy huddles" and don't become what God intends them to be. Circumstances dictated that the four guys who started the fathering group leave and begin another, but this was part of God's plan to challenge the vitality of both groups so they wouldn't become complacent. Sometimes people need to be nudged out of the nest of comfortable familiarity in order to grow. The four guys in the new fathering group admit they grew far more spiritually (they were now in leadership) than if they'd stayed in their comfortable rut, allowing others to do the work.

Setting a New Agenda for the Next Season

Occasionally the change that facilitates group growth is a change in principles and a change of agenda. The members aren't yet ready to divide, but they're ready to graft in a new agenda and work on new principles that will foster spiritual growth. Leaders who are tuned in to their members and tuned in to the Holy Spirit's leading will be able to discern what God is up to in helping their groups to grow.

A mom's-morning-out small group was formed for young mothers dealing with the stress of being on call 24/7 and the continual demands of childcare for infants and toddlers. They were grateful to have an hour to swap stories with one another and know they were not alone in this challenging wedge of their lives. Just having adults to talk with was a treat! But after being together for about nine months, they decided they wanted more than mutual commiseration: They wanted to sink their teeth into something biblically significant. They had gone from the principles of belonging and support to the principles of learning retention and transformation. It took an alert leader to discern that they needed a new agenda in order to move into a new season.

HAVING MEMBERS LEAVE FOR DIFFERENT LEADERSHIP

When we're alert to what God is doing in growing people through small groups, we're sometimes unprepared to see that His next step may be to transplant them into an arena other than small groups. You may remember (chapter 6) that Annette started a "What Now, What Next?" group for women discerning God's leading for the next season of ministry in their lives. Two who attended that group ended up using their gifts in a radically different way.

Both women were artists with a dream of opening a business that combined their love of art with their love for people. One woman provided leadership gifts and the other artistic abilities; both had the gift of hospitality. Together they opened a unique little art-supply shop where people felt safe in exploring their artistic bent in an atmosphere of warm sensitivity and loving support. The women taught classes on various crafts and basic artistic techniques, and those who came felt cared for the first time they entered the shop. As one of the women in this artistic duo put it: "I felt God smile on us as we started this business. We have loved every person as a child of God from the minute they came through the door."

When, with God's leading in mind, we focus on transplanting what needs to grow, we free people to develop in ways that fit how God has wired them. Kevin and Liza first connected in a group for couples with young children. Though they'd attended church faithfully, this was their first small-group experience, and they were a little anxious about what it would be like. It didn't take long for the six young adults in the group to realize they had much in common, and they were soon enjoying a place of support and belonging that they didn't experience in the larger setting of the church's worship service.

In time the group leaders noticed how much Liza loved little children, and they connected her with the children's worship ministry. They also recognized Kevin's incredible service gifts and connected him with the Sunday morning setup team. He loved being a vital part of a group whose work was valued. Kevin and Liza were both transplanted into areas of ministry where their gifts shone; they thrived spiritually and were deeply appreciative of the leaders who supported them. Kevin spoke for both of them when he shared how their group impacted their lives: "I grew up in a Christian home, attended a Christian school, and went to church every week. I had it all up here," he said, pointing to his head. Then he pointed to his heart: "But not until I got involved in this small group did it become a part here."

ALL MEMBERS BECOMING LEADERS

Sometimes God puts people into small groups in order to grow them into leadership for another group. When leaders find themselves leading this kind of "turbo" group, they're intentional about training members in the skills they will need to succeed. Sometimes members of turbo groups lead in one arena and find support in a small group for leaders in another.

REPLACING THE LEADER

Another way to transplant what's growing is by replacing the leader. Some small groups build in leader replacement right from the beginning by requiring an apprentice to be part of the group, someone groomed for future leadership, either in that group or in another. Sometimes leaders need room to grow and feel God leading to another kind of small group or ministry. This happened with Dan and Ginny. After a season of supporting the small group they led, they left to start another kind of group, and another leadership couple took their place.

Sometimes a group member needs to grow and step into leadership. Sometimes several transplanting factors come together at the same time. That's what happened with Cal and Nancy. Together they led a Sunday-morning couples group that radically changed lives; the members were dedicated to growing in their walk with Christ and to serving others. When Mike and Andrea joined, they were each at a very different point on their spiritual journey: Mike was just getting to know Jesus, and Andrea was deeply engaged in her faith commitment. Because of Cal and Nancy's leadership and encouragement, Mike's faith and leadership gifts grew greatly. When Cal and Nancy faced a job transfer to San Francisco, they asked Mike and Andrea to step into leadership in their place. After a time they started another couples group and then another.

Mike got pushed out of the nest a bit prematurely. Sometimes that's how God works to catapult people into spiritual growth. And He moves wonderful leaders, like Cal, out of the way so it can happen. No leader is indispensable. Again, we need to hold the reins of leadership loosely. Sometimes strong leadership inhibits the growth of others' leadership gifts; we need to be careful not to get in the way of what our Creator God wants to grow.

Transplant Timing

In transplanting, timing for added growth is very important. As small groups will need to be transplanted in different ways, they will also be transplanted at different times. Sometimes groups have a slow growth process and the transplanting happens at a later date. These groups will have a second season identical to the first. Actually, a lot of groups will covenant to have two or three identical seasons in a row. Why not?

Things are going well. People are growing in their faith and growing in getting to know one another. Change isn't immediately necessary or even wise.

In both our churches, our pastors did a series of messages on Rick Warren's book *The Purpose-Driven Life,* followed by small-group discussions. Several of those groups decided they wanted to continue to meet for a second season and delve more deeply into the book's concepts, so they maintained the same agenda. Transplanting was premature for them, and those in the group continued to grow by added study on the same subject.

Envisioning Through God's Eyes

God the Creator is in control of all that grows in His garden; we need to be attentive to what He's doing. Some groups will not grow beyond one small group because that's all God intends. Others will be planted in fertile soil so that five or more groups can begin almost immediately. But like the plants in the hanging baskets on my front porch, all small groups need room for their roots. If the roots that we *can't* see are crowded, the plants we *can* see will mirror it. Stunted roots produce stunted plants. Stunted people cannot be productive. That's why transplanting to give room for growth is so critical. Constantly creating new atmospheres for growth, and for releasing people into ministry, safeguards the long-term health of small-group ministry.

When small groups get stuck and need to be challenged to go further, we must pay close attention to what God is doing in them so we can cast His vision for their future. God's vision becomes our vision, and when that happens, we can always anticipate a blessing.

Summary Questions

1. What small groups, small-group leaders, and/or small-group members do you see that may need to be transplanted in order to grow?

2. What needs to happen so that the transplanting process goes well?

3. How can your small groups become more aware of and excited about the importance of transplanting what needs room to grow?

4. What kinds of transplanting have already taken place in your small-group ministry?

5. How will you sharpen your small-group vision so that it includes the transplant process?

CHAPTER NINE:

THE LEADER IS A GARDENER

Barbara kicked off her shoes, put her feet up, and sank deep into the cushions of her favorite chair. She sighed deeply, savoring the spicy warmth of a freshly brewed cup of tea. She was tired. It was good to be home again.

She'd spent the morning attending to the many needs of her small group. Most of them were a little older, and she was grateful she was available for them. She'd grown to love them deeply in the time she'd been their leader.

She smiled to herself as she reflected. The morning had begun with a phone call to Doris; their fifteen-minute chat seemed to ease the loneliness Doris had been feeling after the loss of her husband last year . . . and Barbara ironed three shirts at the same time. Then she drove Grace to her chemotherapy session. After she brought Grace home, Barbara dropped off a prescription at Bill and Carolyn's house and checked in on them. Bill was recovering from back surgery and Carolyn didn't drive—they deeply appreciated Barbara's help and concern.

She sighed. Sometimes the burden of caring for everyone felt heavy. She had such a heart for the elderly, and when she volunteered to lead a church small group for older people, she knew exactly what she was getting into. But it didn't matter to her that their needs would take extra time; God had led her here, and He would provide what she needed.

She also knew she couldn't do everything for her group, and although she did what she could, she was grateful for a wonderful manager/coach who helped to lighten her load. Marie was truly a blessing in Barbara's life. When Barbara first started leading the group, Marie invited her out to lunch, just to get to know her and ask how she could support Barbara's leadership. Together they decided what would be most helpful, and together they set some guidelines, goals, and boundaries for the group. Marie was faithful in prayer support and sent encouraging e-mails every week, some with little tidbits of leadership advice, some with a devotional or Bible verse, and some with a written prayer. Sometimes she just said, "I'm thinking about you today." Barbara felt truly cared for. When Marie asked if she could go with Barbara to visit each member, Barbara was doubly blessed—for herself and for her group members. Sharing the load made it lighter, and she was grateful for the help.

Leaders like Barbara and managers/coaches like Marie know the importance of nurturing people in their faith journey. They understand that small groups are about people, not programs. They intuitively lead in an organic way, rather than in a mechanistic way. They've intentionally developed their small group and small-group ministry by putting people first.

Perhaps at this point we should clarify exactly who we're talking about in terms of roles. Throughout the book, we've talked about three different players in the small-group scene—members, leaders, and managers. *Small-group members* are those who voluntarily join a group, agree on a purpose for being together with others, and commit themselves to accomplishing that purpose together. *Small-group leaders* provide leadership for the group, are responsible for helping the members identify their purpose, and guide the group toward the mutually agreed-upon goal. *Small-group managers* (sometimes called coaches, coordinators, shepherding leaders, resource leaders, etc.) give vision for the entire ministry and empower, train, support, promote, encourage, and oversee the group leaders.

The diagram on page 174 illustrates how all these pieces fit together;

the focus here is on the role of leaders and managers in spiritually developing those under their care. Although leaders and managers work in different circles of care, both are concerned about nurturing the health and growth of the "plants" in their small-group garden—leaders with members, and managers with leaders.

The *manager* acts as the master gardener who oversees multiple gardens and is concerned about the health of the gardeners (leaders) as well as the overall health of each garden (small group). What season are we in? What needs to be started? What plants are mature? What requires special care?

The *leader* is a gardener tending one individual garden, the small group. A gardener, over time, focuses on four primary areas.

First, how is each plant doing? Is it growing and developing as it should? Is it healthy? Does it have enough sun, moisture, nutrients? Is anything attacking it?

Second, how is the overall garden doing? Is it healthy and exciting and looking the way I'd hoped? Is it too crowded? Do I have to transplant anything in it? Is it balanced or out of balance?

Third, how am I as the gardener doing? Do I have enough energy and time to tend the garden? Do I have the resources and equipment to do my job well? How am I developing as a gardener? What unique passions and talents do I see growing in me? (Unhealthy gardeners tend to neglect their gardens, so their health must be safeguarded. This is why having master gardeners who care for the health of the gardeners, as well as the gardens, is so important.)

Fourth, what could be added, changed, or modified in the garden to enhance its productivity and beauty? Do I need to plant new gardens in the landscape? If so, what would that look like?

The Role of the Small-Group Leader as Gardener

As we've mentioned throughout this book, developing people spiritually is a process that takes time and is unique to each person and each group. Because God is the Author and Orchestrator of how people grow, we need to stay close to His heart in order to know how He's growing

His garden. The process of growing people spiritually in a way that He designs includes empowering leaders who understand the vital roles of *praying,* of identifying their small-group *purpose,* and of measuring the *progress* of individuals, the group, and themselves. In growing small groups organically, leaders pay close attention to what's happening so that everyone involved has a chance to grow in a way that honors how and where God is working in their lives. It begins with prayer.

PRAYER: LINKING TO GOD

No matter what your circle of care, prayer—fervent, focused, intentional prayer—is a nonnegotiable for being in leadership. It's foundational. There's no substitute for prayer: It's the least *and* the most leaders can do for those under their care. God moves through the prayers of His people; His power is unleashed through prayer. When we're connected to God through prayer we discern what He's doing and how the Spirit is working in people's lives.

Sam is a small-group leader and trainer who believes in the power of prayer; she quickly admits that without her reliance on God she wouldn't have the confidence to lead a group. It's her closeness to Him that draws her closer to her group members as well—she prays regularly for their spiritual growth and maturity. She's a strong believer in the power of praying Scripture, often using a tool like *Praying the Lord's Prayer for Your Neighbors* (published by HOPE Ministries, available through Faith Alive Christian Resources). She'll also use a Bible passage like Ephesians 3:14–21 and personalize it for each group member. She knows that God responds powerfully to prayer, so she makes it a foundational priority in her leadership role.

Sometimes leaders, though affirming the importance of prayer, find it difficult to find the time in their busy lives to pray for their groups. When they forget to pray, they feel guilty, yet spending time feeling guilty is a waste of time. Instead, leaders can be practical and specific about carving out time to pray. One leader prays for her group members on her way to work every morning; the routine prompts her so she doesn't forget. Another prays during his morning shower. Placing prayer into a daily routine makes it easier to carry out. Be creative; do what fits you as an individual. Those who follow through testify to how connected they feel to the people for whom they pray. God works through prayer, and often the people most changed are those who pray themselves.

Purpose—Covenanting on Why the Group Meets

A second way leaders care for their groups is by being specific and clear about why they're meeting. People are more secure when they know what's what, and covenants are a helpful tool for establishing this. No matter what kind of group, a covenant spells out expectations so that everyone understands why the group is meeting. It's an agreement between members and the leader(s) regarding the who, what, when, why, and how of the small group's existence. This can be a formal written document that everyone signs, or it can be an informal spoken articulation of why the group meets.

Spiritual formation groups might choose a formal covenant simply because accountability is a large piece of their agenda. A relationship-building sports group, on the other hand, may have a much more informal covenant; the leader might simply say, "The purpose of this group is for us to get some physical exercise by batting a ball around and also get to know one another."

One Coffee Break ministry learned the hard way the importance of covenants and pointedly specifying the reason they were meeting. (Recall that Coffee Break is a small-group inductive Bible study for newcomers to the Word, meant to help women develop a personal, vital, growing relationship with Jesus through building loving relationships with others and studying Scripture in a low-key, discover-for-yourself way.) Grace Church began a study with a clear understanding of why they met. God blessed the leaders' desire to reach unchurched neighbors, and they grew greatly.

As they increased, some of the women leading and attending wanted more. "We should provide Christian books for these neighborhood women to read," one leader suggested. It was a great idea, so they started a lending library. Another said, "My group members are ready to dig deeper in our Bible study. We need to provide more commentary background and in-depth Bible study for the women who are growing in their faith." So they added a second level of Bible study. In addition, they added an exercise hour prior to the Bible study as a way to attract more women from the community. Also, they planned special brunches and invited in special speakers.

Ultimately, they added more and more and more until the central purpose for their meeting was lost. These things certainly weren't bad or wrong in and of themselves. The problem was that this Coffee Break didn't have enough leaders to support all they were trying to do, and in exhaustion from trying to be all things to all people, the leaders one by one began to resign.

Eventually the leaders sat down together and asked again, Who are we and why are we meeting? With the guidance and support of their coordinator, they redefined their purpose so it matched with the overall purpose of the Coffee Break ministry. They took ownership for having tried to do too much. Then, both orally and in writing, they clarified their new focus for everyone involved—leaders, attendees, prayer partners, and the supporting congregation—making no apologies for not being everything to everyone.

They admitted they were unable to do all they'd hoped to do, and they experienced great freedom in letting go of the burden of meeting everyone's needs. They also released those who wanted to start other kinds of small groups, encouraging them to do so, and they released attendees who were there for the wrong reasons, pointing them to alternative groups that were a better match for their needs. They freely acknowledged that different people have different needs at different points on their spiritual journey. Being clear about the purpose of Coffee Break helped everyone—leaders and attendees—because each then knew what was expected.

Coffee Break groups have a precisely defined way to grow people. Other kinds of groups provide other ways, but growing people, nevertheless, should be the primary reason *all* small groups exist. The details and context may vary, but the intent is the same: assisting people in becoming all God intends them to be.

PROGRESS: PRINCIPLES AND ONGOING TRAINING

Once leaders define their purpose, they have a standard by which to move on and measure the growth of the individual group members and growth of the group as a whole. One measurement for determining individual or small-group spiritual development is the circle of sociological principles (see the diagram in chapter 5 on page 87) and its correlation with a person's spiritual journey. . . .

Jon was a leader who learned the importance of using this tool. There was a time when the group he was leading wanted to quit; they saw no purpose for meeting anymore. Then Jon brought out the circle of principles and explained them, showing how the principles help people grow spiritually and individually and how they help the whole group grow as well. He asked the members to think about where they were on the circle as individuals. How had their small group helped them grow spiritually? Were they risk-takers? Were they simply sitting on the sidelines, content to just belong as part of the group?

He demonstrated how the principles were not only a way to measure their growth as individuals, but that their group also had a life cycle, capable of development and growth. Together they talked about where they saw their group on the circle. As members caught a vision of what their group could become, they grew more and more excited. In the end, the *group* decided they needed to keep meeting: They had more work to do! They couldn't wait to begin.

Another tool that leaders use to measure the progress of their small group and its members is taking the basic evaluation questions from chapter six and personalizing them for the people under their care. They commit themselves to four goals:

(1) *the growth of each group member;*
(2) *the health and vitality of the group as a whole;*

(3) the balance and health of the leader; and

(4) ways of adding to the small-group ministry.

THE GROWTH OF EACH GROUP MEMBER

People are complex. When we're part of the process of God's growing them on their spiritual journey, we cannot separate their spirituality from who they are as people and all that is going on in their lives. The role of the small-group leader is not to invade people's privacy or break any confidentiality, but in a caring, loving way to assess where they are spiritually and determine the blocks and boosters to helping them grow. Are there wounded, broken places in their lives? What season of life and faith are they in? What's going on around them? What's unique about how God has created them? Our desire as leaders is to connect those under our care more closely to God; that doesn't happen in a vacuum, which is why we need to be acutely aware of the complexities of people's lives.

Don't be overwhelmed by the job: You are *not* solely responsible for each person's health. Instead, responsibly ask, Is this person being cared for? Other members of the group might provide support, and sometimes outside resources and counseling may be needed. Our primary concern is to address these life issues in order to provide an environment for helping members grow spiritually. Are they getting to know God more deeply? Are they maturing in character, in values, and in relationships? Do they know their spiritual gifts, and are they using them in service and vocation as well as in developing a Christian worldview? How can we help provide a safe, nurturing environment in which they can thrive?

Hal took seriously his role of nurturing the faith of his group members; he was tuned in to signs of their spiritual growth. Kevin joined Hal's small group, having little connection to the church. Though he believed in God, he had little awareness of what it means to have a personal relationship with Christ. Hal accepted Kevin exactly where he was in his spiritual journey. He invested in Kevin personally, getting to know him, his values, and his interests. He provided a safe place for Kevin to ask his questions about God and the Bible. He patiently listened without judging Kevin or requiring a "right" response. And in God's timing and the nurturing environment that Hal provided in their Bible study, Kevin not only committed his life to Christ but he also grew in his faith by leaps and bounds. In many ways, even though he'd been spiritually behind other members of the group at the outset, Kevin moved around the circle of principles before many of the others did.

Hal encouraged his growth and provided resources to help him grow; he saw leadership gifts in Kevin and affirmed them. When Hal moved to another city to take a new job, he asked Kevin to replace him as leader of the group. It was then, more than ever, that Kevin grew in his faith and his leadership gifts became evident. Sometimes one leader has to leave to make room for another. Hal didn't leave *because* Kevin was emerging as a leader, but he was wise in discerning that God was preparing Kevin to take his place. Providing specific ways to nurture the faith of each member is an important part of growing people in small groups.

Kevin's story is only one of many from their group. Others also joined with various kinds of brokenness in their lives, some emotional and some spiritual, and one by one they found healing and growth. As they did, they likewise moved into different kinds of leadership—one as an elder, others as deacons, and still others as small-group leaders. God used Hal to start a process of spiritual growth that continued long after he moved away.

When people become our focus, we become attentive to their uniqueness; we fulfill our purpose of growing them in their faith journey by sharing with them the gifts we observe, nurturing those gifts, and encouraging their use. We applaud the diversity of personalities, delighting in who they are and what they contribute to the whole body. In time, we might connect them to a resource that helps them become more aware of the next step God may have in mind. One beneficial tool is *LifeKeys* (by Jane Kise, David Stark, and Sandra Hirsh), which broadly helps people identify their personality types, life gifts, spiritual gifts, passions, and values. Faith Alive Christian Resources has a spiritual-gifts inventory, *Discover Your Gifts*, which is also very helpful from a narrower perspective. (Information on these tools is listed in the back of this book.) Defining both broadly and narrowly why small groups are important builds trust between leaders/managers and their respective circles of care.

THE HEALTH AND VITALITY OF THE GROUP AS A WHOLE

The health and growth of the group itself is also a priority. Are its relationships growing deeper? Has its quality increased? Is there progression from one principle to another as appropriate to the type of group? Are members committed to the group and motivated to be involved? Are we growing in our discipleship? What are we primarily doing together? Am I as a leader equipping my group members as I should?

Because growth patterns vary among members, leaders must be attentive to the health and vitality of the entire group, not just the growth of its individuals. Ironically, in some cases one or two individuals may grow spiritually by leaps and bounds and yet the group as a whole is unhealthy. In fact, sometimes uneven individual growth hinders the larger group from being healthy and moving forward.

One member of a men's group was passionate about being an evangelist to his brother-in-law, who was also in the group. The brother-in-law was just beginning to discover Jesus, cautiously exploring what it means to build relationships with committed Christian men. On the other hand, three or four other members wanted to move past the relationship-building stage and get into life transformation. They expressed how they felt about the group's direction by simply not showing up or disengaging and refusing to participate fully. It took an alert leader and manager to discern what was happening and divide the group into two in order to satisfy the needs of both sides. One part became a men's group to reach those who were exploring Christianity, and the other became a group for on-fire believers living out their faith in life-transforming ways. Without that division, the original group would surely have atrophied and died.

THE BALANCE AND HEALTH OF THE LEADER

Leaders need to check their pulse and take their temperature from time to time. Am I spiritually and emotionally healthy? To whom am I accountable in this regard? What season of life am I in? What motivates me as a leader? What passions, talents, and gifts are growing in me? What training do I need? Are there issues in my life that are hindering my leadership? How am I growing spiritually?

Because concern for people is primary, leaders need people who support them and are concerned for their health and growth. Everyone needs to be accountable to someone, and everyone needs to be an encourager and supporter of others. Each person's growth needs will be unique: It may be as basic as having a listening ear or praying with someone, it may be linking a leader to a helpful book, or it may be as difficult as recognizing that a leader is in crisis and encouraging him or her to step down for a time.

Kathy had a sensitive manager who did exactly that. Kathy was one of David's best discipleship leaders, and people loved being in her small group—they were drawn closer to God as she made the Bible come alive. Then Kathy went through the stress and strain of infertility. Her group members began to reflect her own struggle in their faith-walk as well. Instead of being drawn closer to Christ, they began to question God and expressed anger at how He was working in their lives. David perceived what was happening with Kathy and with her group members. In loving concern, he suggested that perhaps she needed some time away in order to sort out the issues in her life.

Kathy and David had a relationship of mutual respect, and when he gently confronted her with what was taking place, she readily agreed to a temporary break from leadership. Eventually she joined an infertility support group, and, in working through the pain of being unable to have a baby, she also found God again, seeing His faithfulness and love in her life. Stepping away for a season was what she needed to become healthy and well.

David provided just the kind of care Kathy needed. Care for others cannot be done in cookie-cutter fashion, so leaders of leaders stay closely in tune with God's heart in order to know how best to serve those under their care.

Leaders should always keep their eyes, ears, and hearts attuned to new growth opportunities. In the case of the men's group mentioned above, not only did the division ensure the health of the group, but it added to the growth of the small-group ministry as a whole by adding another group. But growth could also mean sponsoring a new group or sending out a new leader. Sometimes growth happens when members testify to others about the importance of a small group in their lives, encouraging new people to get involved. Growth might mean moving from leading a group to becoming a manager.

Once again, growing things are not static but dynamic, so we always need to ask, What is God doing in our group and in the ministry as a whole? Where is the Holy Spirit at work and causing growth? For the growth of the entire garden of small groups, we may need to thin, transplant, and plant new seeds from new opportunities, all with a clear view not to what we desire but to where we see God already at work.

The Role of the Small-Group Manager as Master Gardener

You've probably noticed that the last two areas we've discussed—the balance and health of the leader, and adding to the small-group ministry—include the role of the manager as well as the leader. It was David's wise intervention that kept Kathy and her group from crashing, and it is the manager's role to oversee and provide proper opportunity for new groups that form. Managers free small-group leaders from administrative detail so they can concentrate on care.

But make no mistake: Small groups aren't first of all about administrative details, even for managers—they're about growing people. Managers too are primarily concerned about the people (leaders) under their immediate care. Everything we've shared about the role of small-group leaders in nurturing their members likewise pertains to managers and their care of leaders. If you're a manager and you've skipped over this part, please consider going back and reading it. *Growing people is primary;* all that we do administratively is in support of this. Structures serve the people; people don't serve structures.

However, the role of being a leader of leaders in growing people through small groups also has overarching responsibilities that being a leader of a small group does not. In addition to being attentive to the health and growth of the leaders under their care, managers fill roles that impact the entire ministry. They're the vision-casters for small groups, and they're the people who interpret the community, helping to determine what people need. Managers ensure leaders get the training they need to do their job well, and they're trained themselves to be living examples of how small groups help people grow spiritually. Managers also are the ambassadors for small groups in the larger church structure, making sure the interests of small-group ministry are protected, understood, and developed. They're problem-solvers and facilitators in times of conflict. They oversee the overall health of the ministry.

VISION-CASTER

Casting vision for small groups and the role they play in people's spiritual growth is a vital part of a manager's role. He or she helps people to see the possibilities God has in store for them down the road and compels them to join the work to get there. With a strong foundation of prayer, fingers on the pulse of the community, and a clear understanding of how the small-group nesting vision fits into the church's overall vision, the small-groups manager constantly sets new directions for the small-group ministry. In a smaller church, the manager helps discern how to narrow the focus of small groups so they can become successful in meeting people's needs without exhausting the church's people resources by spreading them too thin. In a large church, the manager may see just the right time to launch small groups out of their Gen-X service, for example, or when a sermon series is an opening to invite people to participate. These leaders with an eye on the future act as master gardeners, seeing multiple gardens in full bloom while scattering seeds in the wind for others to nurture and cultivate. Every season they oversee the process of resetting vision. Although they manage what is, they live also in a what-will-be world.

INTERPRETER OF THE COMMUNITY

The manager's vision, however, is liberally sprinkled with a large dose of reality. Again, they ask, what is God doing in our church community? How is He working in the community around us? What does He want us to see? What needs does He want us to meet? What seeds does He want us to plant? What needs watering? What needs pruning? What needs fertilizing? What needs to be grafted into something else that's vibrant and growing?

When I (David) started as our church's small-groups pastor, I began with interpreting our community. When I asked, "What is God up to in this or that part of our church?" I found many answers. First, I looked at a number of renewal groups that had been meeting for a long time. They had no trained leadership, no covenants for evaluating why they were meeting and whether they were achieving what they'd hoped. I recognized these groups were longstanding and were important to the people in them; to interfere by setting a whole new list of expectations would accomplish nothing but hard feelings, so I let them be. What I did instead was form groups around them, groups that started out with a covenant and whose leaders were trained to lead. After a period of time, those longstanding groups atrophied to just having breakfast together. But vibrant spiritual renewal groups were now in place too, and people had an opportunity to have their need for growth met there.

I also checked out our Circle of Friends groups, the largest kind of small group at the time. There were between one hundred and two hundred people involved with these once-a-month glorified dinner parties (with almost no spiritual content). Once again, as I discerned what God was doing, I nudged them forward. I knew the dinner groups were a great beginning place where people could get to know one another, but I also wanted them to have a vision of moving people into deeper sorts of principle-based, covenant-based small groups. Over time I helped the dinner-group leaders discern their role and begin to build bridges to deeper kinds of groups as well.

Our seniors small groups also needed some refinement, but not in a heavy-handed way. I encouraged their coach/manager to simply love them, support them, affirm the many good things they were doing, and invite them to our small-group training. We also explained that not all our women's small groups would look exactly like those they already had in place; we began other kinds of women's groups as well. Over time all the groups began to take advantage of our training and be involved with our management. What could have become divisive instead became unifying, simply because we honored the community we were serving.

Interpreting the community isn't limited to what's happening in the church community, however; we also need to interpret what's happening in the community around us. In fact, usually the interpretation of the community is in pockets of people inside or outside the church that don't have small groups. You may remember the story of Jessica, who started a program for latchkey kids in her downtown church's neighborhood. She was an interpreter of her community, and out of that program she eventually started groups that embraced the children's parents as well. The support group Janet led was also started because someone recognized that many people in the community were dealing with grief and loss. The mothers-of-teens group that surrounded Susan with love and support when her son took his life reached out to women just like her, women who denied God's existence but then found Him through the love of a small group.

Interpreting the community means being sensitive to both inreach small groups and outreach small groups. Inreach groups specifically target believers; outreach small groups target those just beginning their spiritual journey. Each has both an inside and an outside focus.

An inreach small group with an inside focus is for believers who are members of the sponsoring church. An inreach small group with an outside focus is also for committed Christians, but for those who are not currently members of the sponsoring church. An outreach small group with an inside focus targets people who are part of a church (they may even be members) but who stay on the outer fringe of body life and have never committed their lives to Christ. An outreach small group with an outside focus aims to draw in those who are just beginning to explore their faith-walk or have some other pressing need.

Understanding the differences between inreach and outreach small groups is helpful in determining where people are focusing their energy. Without an outreach component to infuse new life at some point, we miss the blessings God gives when we obey His command to "make disciples of all nations," beginning right where we are.

Tom and Julie discovered this. When they first joined a small group with four other couples, they felt life had finally become complete for them—living in authentic community with other couples was the piece that had been missing from their lives, and the others felt the same way. They were ecstatic; they did everything together from prayer to worship to leisure activities. Their families even vacationed together. So when I (Betty) met Tom in the grocery store, not having seen anyone from their group for at least a year, I wasn't prepared for what he shared. I knew how close their group had been, and in the course of catching up on our lives I was eager to hear how they were doing. "Oh, that!" he grimaced. "That died long ago, and when it did, it died a bloody death."

I hurt for the pain I knew everyone must have felt. Something had gone terribly wrong. There certainly may have been several contributing factors, but primarily all their energy had been focused inward; energy that has no outward focus tends to implode, and that's what happened to their group. They became too myopic, and because they had no channel for outreach, they self-destructed. When interpreting the community around us, we need to provide small-group balance between inreach and outreach.

PROVIDER OF TRAINING

Maybe what happened to Tom and Julie's group could have been avoided if they'd had the necessary training to stay healthy. The church they'd been part of when they first started their group disbanded, but they continued to meet without any oversight. Accountability and evaluation are important; so important, in fact, that we don't just talk about organic small groups based on principles, we have leadership training workshops to teach about them. *Launch and Lead Your Own Small Group* gives foundational instruction on getting started; the *Next Steps* small-groups workshop is an evaluation tool for groups that have been meeting for some time and need to assess their health and determine their future. (Information on both can be found in the back of this book.) Other types of training may also be valuable as needs arise.

Effective organic managers are constantly training new leaders. In the years that I (David) have worked as a small-groups pastor, I've found that I'll probably launch about 50 percent of the people I train as leaders, roughly a two-to-one ratio. If I want to launch ten groups, I need to train twenty leaders. If I want forty, I need eighty in training. Some end up being delayed launches and will begin a year or two after they get trained, but the guideline still applies. Training equips people for leadership and is essential because it provides the tools leaders need to serve well.

Ongoing training may be as simple and informal as providing e-mail leadership tips or notes of encouragement, or it may be more structured. Sometimes there's no substitute for simple visuals. When Lois used a tennis ball to show how to guide a healthy discussion, the lesson stuck in ways that words alone could not have conveyed. She formed a circle of leaders and she, as the group's leader, held the ball. She tossed it to someone, they tossed it back to her, and she repeated the back-and-forth toss with everyone in the group. All eyes were on her; she held their focus. Then she asked them to toss the ball to one another. Occasionally she got the ball, but so did everyone else. They needed to pay attention to each other, not just to the leader. The group became more animated and interactive. After the exercise they evaluated what had happened. They understood in a whole new way how the leader acts as a facilitator rather than controller of the discussion. They could take what they learned and immediately practice it.

Again, Jon uses the circle of principles as a training tool; he's found that it stretches and challenges his small-group leaders. He asks each of them, "What principle are you working on?" Together they talk about how to move the group forward or, if the group's purpose is limited in scope, how to nudge members forward in their spiritual journey by either getting involved in other kinds of groups or becoming a group leader. His leaders are open to his leadership because he invests in them. They know he prays faithfully for them. They see him personally model what he believes. He walks alongside them and encourages them. He provides the training and resources they need to do their job well. He makes their job easier, not harder. He wants them to succeed. Training, whether simple or comprehensive, makes better leaders.

AMBASSADOR

Another essential role for the manager of a small-group ministry is that of ambassador. Being an ambassador is more than building goodwill about small groups through publicity and promotional information, though it certainly includes that. It especially (and essentially) involves making the stories of changed lives and exciting growth known to the congregation and the staff. Let them know the positives that are happening. Videotape transformational stories from small groups. Inform people of the breadth and depth of the ministry as a whole. But mostly, just tell stories. Everyone loves stories—they're living, breathing illustrations of God at work in His garden.

I (David) know how well this works. I just finished thirteen years on staff at Christ Presbyterian Church, and for the better part of the decade in which we tracked our small-group ministry, we had an average of 22 percent small-group growth per year. We had no single moment of big launches. We just consistently kept raising the banner of small groups, telling the stories of changed lives, and steadily, slowly, we added groups a few at a time, following God where we saw Him at work, until soon we had a fully developed ministry.

After a decade, around 92 percent of the congregation was involved in groups. If we factored in our task forces as well, 111 percent of those attending worship were involved in groups. That number is only possible, of course, because through our small groups we're reaching people in our community that aren't currently part of our worshiping body. Yea, God!

Mechanistic models may be able to manipulate numbers for a time, but organic ministry works long-term because the people in it are transformed.

PROBLEM-SOLVER

Small groups, though, are *not* about numbers. They're about people, people who laugh and love and grow and are endearing—and who sometimes make things very messy. That's why another crucial role the small-group manager plays is that of being a problem-solver or trouble-shooter. Managers help leaders succeed. Sometimes this means simply being available to listen, to be a sounding board, to ask reflective questions and guide leaders in finding the answers to their own questions. The majority of a manager's time, about 75 percent, is spent simply praying for, supporting, and loving the leaders under his or her care. The other 25 percent is spent coaching leaders in the four evaluation questions and the four goals for small groups (see chapter seven). *All* of the time—100 percent—is spent in putting people first and helping them grow in their walk as a leader and in their walk with Christ. When we truly enter into people's lives, God works in amazing ways. Most often things go well in small groups when the leaders are healthy and growing.

LIVING EXAMPLE

People often mirror what they experience. It takes being in a group to be authentic regarding what group life is all about, so being part of a small group is nonnegotiable for a manager. Being a living example, though, includes more than what a manager *does;* it's who a manager *is.* Managers who love their leaders raise up leaders who love their group members. This is essential for successfully overseeing a small-group ministry. It's through being a living example that managers understand the power and dynamics of group life.

Now, having said all we have about the roles of small-group leaders and managers and how they lead, we need to add one more thing. These people are human, flawed, imperfect, weak, and in most ways no different from the people they both lead and serve. And if they're healthy themselves, they'll be secure enough to let the people they lead know it.

Small groups aren't successful because they have perfect people leading them; they're successful because God is in charge. Remember the continuum of spiritual growth we bounce around on our journey to becoming completely committed Christ-followers? Well, hopefully we get a little wiser with each step along the way. And the wiser we get, the more we reflect to others the love of God that we ourselves are grasping in a greater way each day.

God is love. We love because He first loved us. Love is the glue that holds small groups together. Small-group members love their groups because they feel loved there. They follow imperfect leaders when those leaders love them. Love, more than any other factor, holds small groups together. Whether it's love for a cause, or love for a common commitment to an agenda, or simply love for one another, the fertilizer that grows small groups is love. Above all, "love each other deeply, because love covers over a multitude of sins" (1 Peter 4:8).

Summary Questions

1. What should a leader look for in his or her group members in order to be sensitive to their needs in the group? What specific things can a leader do to encourage their spiritual and personal growth?

2. What, if anything, would you as a leader change, emphasize, or stop doing if you led according to the needs of your group members and the group as a whole, rather than according to a planned agenda or curriculum?

3. What do you see as the greatest challenge in motivating an entire small group to grow?

4. What have you learned from reading about the various roles of the small-group manager(s)? Which roles are most apparent in your small-groups ministry? Which need greater emphasis?

5. What do you think it would take in your church to make your small groups be all God intends them to be? What steps might you take to get there?

CHAPTER TEN:

THE LEADER AS SHEPHERD

Pastor John knew his church's small groups were in trouble. He'd seen the decline both in the numbers of groups and in how many people attended them. Leaders were dropping out left and right, and the entire ministry was at a crossroads. As senior pastor, John discussed the situation with the church leadership: Either they needed to scrap their small groups, or they needed to revitalize them in a whole new way.

At that point, Greg, the staff person in charge of small groups, introduced the leaders to principle-based groups. Together they became convinced of the importance of releasing people to dream God's dreams; this made more sense than the model-based approach they'd been trying to implement, and they wanted to begin again.

As a staff member, Greg also knew that the change would work best if the pastor supported it. This was markedly different from the reports and systems that had been part of the cookie-cutter approach they'd been using. It meant trusting others and giving up control, even if it meant a certain amount of risk of failure.

Because Pastor John had already seen the grim statistics on their small-group ministry, he was open when Greg suggested a new direction. At Greg's suggestion, he attended the training on principle-based small groups and became involved in a group himself. It was a stretch, of course, so he eased into the scene gradually. First he started with a one-on-one mentoring group studying Henry Blackaby's *Experiencing God*, an intense spiritual accountability group that he found both challenging and rewarding. He also became involved in a couples fellowship group with his wife. Then he added a men's breakfast-and-Bible-study group. When the mentoring group ended, he started a new group based on his own passion, physical fitness, inviting other guys who were early risers like himself to join a FIT (Fitness In Training) group.

Through three very different kinds of small groups, Pastor John experienced for himself the benefits of releasing people to use their gifts rather than recruiting them to fill positions. He grew personally, and the church's small-group ministry grew as well. He saw the energy created and released when people were empowered; he learned the joy of giving away ministry. His enthusiasm permeated his messages on Sunday mornings and his interaction with others all week long. "The senior pastor can't do everything," he said, "but you don't speak passionately about something unless you're involved." Because he became involved in small groups himself, Pastor John became passionate about empowering others to embrace them as well. Looking back at the point where principle-based groups got started, he offered this insight: "Until small groups became a major influence in the ministry and care of our church—not just something on the side—small groups struggled." Today they're vibrant—growing people in the way God intended.

This pastor learned some important lessons along the way. First, he learned he couldn't do everything and that God equips the body of believers to work together, each contributing his own gifts to benefit the whole. Releasing others to use their unique gifts uplifts the whole body. Second, he learned that he needed to either carry the vision for small groups or authorize someone else to carry it. In his case, he did both: He had a passion for small groups because of his personal involvement, but he also recognized his own limitations, so he empowered Greg and the leaders in the small-group ministry to use their gifts. Finally, he learned that providing nurture and care through small groups was a key component to the spiritual growth of his congregation.

Basically, Pastor John's church moved from a small-group ministry based on a curriculum and a list of requirements—a mechanistic model—to an organic model that released the gifts and passions of others, enabling them to use their God-given gifts. Instead of leading from a position of power and control, he led by creating an atmosphere of trust and nurture. He saw his leaders as saints, people who were new creations in Christ, rather than as sinners or people whose flaws needed to be controlled. He followed the Ezekiel 34 vision for leadership—the kind that is badly needed today. It is a leadership that leads to life transformation and enfolds organic small groups into body life.

This leadership focuses on people's potential, not on their brokenness; on the unique creations they are, not on the slot they can fill in a church program. Jesus focused on the potential of Peter the "rock," not the imperfect man who denied him three times. He saw Peter through the grid of grace and redemption, releasing him to be a church builder (Matthew 16:18). He also empowered Paul to be a missionary, who in his own words was "less than the least of all God's people, [but] this grace was given me: to preach to the Gentiles the unsearchable riches of Christ" (Ephesians 3:8). The man who had persecuted Christ's followers became a leader in transforming their lives. These and many others throughout the New Testament illustrate Christ's desire that we see people through the eyes of His redeeming love, not as people who need to be micromanaged and controlled.

This biblical image is quite different from the leadership models that some church leaders use today. They've adapted an outdated business model that emphasizes power and control rather than empowerment and nurture. These are leaders who are more concerned about advancing their own agenda and being followed than they are about caring for others. The Old Testament had leaders like that too, and God (through Ezekiel) had strong words for them:

> *Woe to the shepherds of Israel who only take care of themselves!*
> *Should not shepherds take care of the flock? . . . You have not*
> *strengthened the weak or healed the sick or bound up the injured. You*
> *have not brought back the strays or searched for the lost. You have*
> *ruled them harshly and brutally. So they were scattered because there*
> *was no shepherd, and when they were scattered they became food for*
> *all the wild animals. . . . They were scattered over the whole earth,*
> *and no one searched or looked for them. (34:2, 4–6)*

God is not indifferent to how His sheep are treated:

> *I am against the shepherds and will hold them accountable for*
> *my flock. I will remove them from tending the flock so that the shep-*
> *herds can no longer feed themselves. I will rescue my flock from their*
> *mouths, and it will no longer be food for them. . . . I myself will*
> *search for my sheep and look after them. (34:10–11)*

God makes very clear what He wants from the leaders of His flock, the church of Jesus Christ: Take care of His sheep.

In this book we've talked at length about leadership. By God's grace, some national church leaders have put it back on the map for the church: They've recognized that leadership is of major importance, and that churches deserve and need to be led—not just given pastoral care and taught—but truly led. The problem is that much of the available leadership literature doesn't reflect the Bible's message about specific kinds of leadership. There is a definite pattern of commandments around the leadership that Jesus discussed regarding the building of God's kingdom. Some kinds of leadership aren't scriptural and are actually condemned in various places.

What Biblical Leadership Is Not

In keeping with the Ezekiel passage, leadership that looks to its own interests first is not biblical leadership. In Philippians 2:3–7 we're challenged:

Do nothing out of selfish ambition or vain conceit, but in humility consider others better than yourselves. Each of you should look not only to your own interests, but also to the interests of others. Your attitude should be the same as that of Christ Jesus: Who, being in very nature God, did not consider equality with God something to be grasped, but made himself nothing, taking the very nature of a servant.

First Peter 5:2–3 spells it out clearly as well:

Be shepherds of God's flock that is under your care, serving as overseers—not because you must, but because you are willing, as God wants you to be; not greedy for money, but eager to serve; not lording it over those entrusted to you, but being examples to the flock.

Self-serving leaders hinder the spiritual development of God's people, and the results are disastrous.

First, like the sheep in Ezekiel 34, the people scatter. They know when they're not being cared for and they look elsewhere, sometimes in good places, sometimes in not-so-good places.

Second, turf battles take place. Power is an incredible lure: once people have it, they don't easily give it up and, in fact, usually deal with a desire for just a little bit more. People who have it work to protect it; people take sides, and the people with the most power "win." When that happens, the church has some "fat sheep" and some "lean sheep" (Ezekiel 34). Special interests arise, favoritism is rampant, and those with little power and little voice are neglected and become spiritually malnourished.

Finally, Satan attacks the sheep because they're scattered and wandering. They scatter because the leadership is harsh and controlling; the flock can't live up to the expectations placed on them. They find that they've exchanged one list of requirements for being "good enough" (the world's) for another set of rules for being "good enough" (the church's).

They feel cajoled and controlled, not nurtured and nourished. This kind of leadership is a hindrance, not a help, to spiritual transformation.

What Biblical Leadership Is

What, then, is the pastor's role in creating vital small groups that grow people? A fundamental challenge to many popular leadership images of recent years is the biblical mandate to be a shepherd. This is a relational image, not a structural or positional one. Pastors, and all leadership staff, need to take their cues from the Good Shepherd.

God as shepherd responds quite differently to us than the shepherds talked about in Ezekiel 34. He does not use control and command; He tends the sheep. His focus is on health, vitality, and growth. He seeks the lost and brings them into green pasture so they can grow, blossom, and be nourished.

God as shepherd also rules justly over other leaders to make sure the fat sheep are not given advantage over the lean sheep. He holds leaders accountable to *fairly* (not always *equally*) distribute resources so that at the right time every sheep has what it takes to grow. He protects those who are undernourished or malnourished because of leaders who act in manipulative and personally ambitious ways. He replaces the goal of compliance through command and control with the goals of spiritual accountability and growth through trust and support.

Leadership that begins with a core of trust supports its people and yet is also accountable for leading them to greater growth. Leading like the Good Shepherd isn't non-leadership: it's leadership that cares about people, that truly loves deeply those entrusted to one's care, always stretching people to the next level of spiritual growth in a way that honors where God is at work.

Practical Implications for Senior Pastors and Pastoral Staff

Following the example of Jesus the Good Shepherd means pastors and staff members need to take specific, proactive, practical steps.

PRAY

Remember: It begins with prayer. Jesus spent many hours in prayer with His Father, sometimes staying up all night; He drew apart to be alone in prayer (see Matthew 14:23; Mark 1:35; Luke 6:12). It was in oneness with His Father that He died to His own desires and submitted to the Father's will (Matthew 26:42).

If small-group leaders and managers need to pray, how much more their pastors? God makes very clear that leaders are held to a higher standard: James (3:1) warns us that "not many of you should presume to be teachers, my brothers, because you know that we who teach will be judged more strictly." Spiritual discernment is crucial for leading with authenticity and integrity, which come from being close to God's heart in prayer. At the core of ministry is the Holy Spirit's move upon God's people. In the church's goal of spiritual growth and transformation, its spiritual leaders simply endeavor to follow God's lead and then create an atmosphere where people can flourish within the bounds of spiritual accountability.

Leadership carries with it the weight of responsibility, and many pastors and pastoral staff are tempted to try controlling people and outcomes. However, they must hold to their leadership loosely, trusting God with the results and resting in His leading. Pastors should never move forward any faster than they can go on their knees.

CAST THE VISION

In order to create that atmosphere of trust and empowerment, the pastor needs to be a *visionary*. This doesn't necessarily mean pastors personally carry out the vision for organic small groups (though they may), but that they adopt a vision big enough so that the individual visions of various leaders or sub-ministries can fit under it. Again: Either the pastor carries the vision, or the pastor empowers someone else to carry the vision and provides support. Pastors near to God's heart may be personally wired to control, but they'll have the discipline to surrender that tendency because the Spirit has given them a vision beyond themselves and taught them to trust His leading.

CREATE AN ATMOSPHERE OF TRUST

Remember the organic imagery we've used all along for what's necessary to grow people spiritually? It applies to pastoral leadership as well. Pastors must create an atmosphere of trust before people will feel empowered and the small-group ministry can thrive. They do this in three ways:

(1) *by establishing core values;*
(2) *by safeguarding the interests of everyone; and*
(3) *by empowering the gifts of others.*

- *Establishing Core Values*

The first step to creating an atmosphere of trust is setting boundaries. People need to know where they stand in order to feel safe enough to trust. As we've said, in an organic structure, it's not "anything goes." The church's vision and mission is the heart of what the church is called to do, so it sets the boundaries. The core values arise out of the church's vision statement; the small-groups nesting vision fits inside the church's mission; all the different kinds of groups fit inside the nesting vision.

Pastors need to be clear in establishing core biblical values and then asking the leadership to commit themselves to being accountable to them. These core values need to reflect the image of the body in 1 Corinthians 12. We recognize that *we're better together* (synergy); we need one another. When one rejoices, we all rejoice; when one suffers, we all suffer. We will have *trust-based, supportive, accountable relationships* because we recognize that we're all part of the same body. We'll be *collaborative* because we work best when each contributes a vital part. We'll look to *the good of the whole,* not just to our individual interests and agendas. We'll honor the lesser parts of the body.

- *Safeguarding the Interests of Everyone*

Honoring the lesser parts of the body means pastors need to safeguard the interests of everyone. Pastors don't have the luxury of playing favorites if they're committed to leading biblically. Again, God gave Ezekiel harsh words for shepherds who were feeding the fat sheep, who merely became fatter, and starved the lean sheep. Pastors need to lift up the downtrodden, protect their rights as children of God, and responsibly apportion resources to everyone.

Pastors need to acknowledge they're not completely objective. They too have special interests and in their position of authority could abuse them. They need to be accountable so that they lead justly.

The field of communication says no person is objective. *Standpoint theory* says everyone has a standpoint from which he or she interprets the world around them. We may have a Christian standpoint, a male or female standpoint, an ethnic standpoint, a divorced-person standpoint, a single standpoint, and so on. Most probably have combinations of standpoints. The point is, none of us is objective. All of us (and particularly those in positions of power) need to be careful not to buy into one standpoint, whether it's ours or someone else's. The *only* standpoint leaders may buy into is that of Christ Jesus, for He looks to the interests of others.

This might mean that the senior pastor dies to his own agenda from time to time when discerning that the Spirit is blessing the passions of others. The pastor recognizes turf protection and the lobbying of special interest groups within the church. The pastor acts justly toward all, making sure that the proper resources are allocated to those who need them, that various associate pastors and ministries are respected and given a voice. Bias and partiality are avoided.

Leading in a spirit of humility is Christlike. So is putting the needs of others before our own. Growing people God's way requires this kind of leadership, leadership that fights for those who cannot fight for themselves. It means responsibly nurturing people on their faith journey, often simply by empowering those who are gifted to provide that nurture.

- *Empowering the Gifts of Others*

Empowering gifts in others is the third part of creating a trust-filled atmosphere. Jesus empowered others, and He did it before they were really ready. If He had waited for the Twelve to "get it right," He'd never have entrusted the spread of the gospel to them. But He allowed them to do it imperfectly. Pastors need to be empowering like Jesus; *that* elicits trust. Empowering pastors give those in charge of the small-group ministry the freedom to explore where God is at work. In an empowering climate of trust, when individual leaders have visions, they aren't snuffed out or immediately controlled. When those visions fit within the nesting vision, they're encouraged and supported. Individual gifts are drawn out, and people are empowered to use them. Sometimes empowerment happens in ways that stretch the body.

When Pastor Doug empowered his small-group ministry to adopt an organic, principle-based approach, he knew it was a radical change in thinking, but he didn't anticipate exactly how it would upset the comfortable world of his congregation. One thing he truly appreciated was the enthusiasm and clarity Sam brought to the leadership-training workshop she conducted for those interested in leading groups. The church was buzzing with the excitement of creating new kinds of groups out of people's gifts and passions; there was a new energy as the church began reaching outside its walls and building bridges to the community.

It also caused a bit of a fuss, though, and Pastor Doug heard about it soon enough. He called Sam to let her know: "We have a problem in our small groups, and it's your fault."

Sam's heart raced; she wondered what could have happened, so she listened as Pastor Doug told the story. Apparently a couple of guys with a heart for reaching their buddies decided to start a bowling group, inviting a few of their friends to join them. It was a low-key, relationship-building kind of group, and it worked—a few of their friends joined. Then the church elders received word that a couple of these guys were drinking beer while they bowled. They brought it to the attention of the board of elders at their next meeting. Since Pastor Doug had supported this new way of doing small groups, the elders held him responsible: "What are you going to do about it?" they wanted to know. Their high-control, top-down radar was on full alert. This was a crisis.

Sam felt the crisis as well, and her heart beat faster as she waited for

Pastor Doug to unload on her. Instead, he laughed. He was delighted with the problem; it was evidence that the church had broken out of its cloistered shell and was reaching people who needed to be reached. He couldn't wait to share with Sam what was happening, and he thanked her for bringing a spark of evangelistic fervor back into their congregation.

Pastor Doug was a wise leader. In response to the elders' question as to what he was going to do about the beer at the bowling groups, he simply said, "Nothing." Except, he told them, he intended to support the church's small-group manager and the bowling-group leaders, so they in turn could nurture their people. He held leadership loosely, but he held the command to reach the lost seriously.

The church's vision and core values were clearly stated; each leader understood the small-group nesting vision and was committed to supporting it. All the leaders had been trained, and un-empowering them would have reversed the progress they'd made in implementing organic small groups. Pastor Doug knew what he risked in responding to the board of elders as he did, but he'd also created an atmosphere of trust with them and believed they could weather this storm together. They'd been a part of the decision to implement an organic small-group structure—this was an opportunity to test their choice. He knew the importance of personal modeling in his leadership role, and he intended to live out the church leadership's commitment.

MODEL IT

Anything pastors might say about empowerment and freedom is empty without behavior that backs it up. Remember the old sayings "practice what you preach" and "actions speak louder than words"? Both pack a wallop in small-group ministry. Pastors can't avoid these; they're on center stage, and the people around them quickly perceive when what they say is inconsistent with how they live. It's fairly easy to be an empowering leader when everything is going smoothly, but what happens in times of crisis? Will pastors have the courage to support those they've empowered, or will they slip into default mode and seize control?

Though there are times "default mode" may be necessary in order to protect the church, leaders should resort to it sparingly. It's also true that sometimes the senior pastor is able to do something better than some of the small-group leaders. But while Jesus would always be able to do everything better than His disciples, He walked alongside them, modeling for them and promising never to leave them. Pastors also need to walk alongside the managers, modeling for them and empowering them to release people to use their God-given gifts, trusting the Holy Spirit's guidance throughout their journey together.

No one suggests that the role of senior pastor or any pastoral support staff is easy. Many today are part of denominational and ecclesiastical structures that are laden with political infighting, bureaucracy, and turf protection. When Patrick Lencioni shared his *Five Dysfunctions of a Team* at Willow Creek's Leadership Summit in August 2003, you could have heard a pin drop. Everybody knew that building relationships with staff, long-term, is an enormously difficult thing to do. It requires spiritual maturity to be a group of people that constantly looks to the whole, that constantly denies itself.

Some senior pastors are truly good leaders, *servant* leaders, yet still struggle with their role in organic small-group ministry. "It's not that I can't empower other leaders," one shared. "I simply feel so responsible for the care of my congregation, and I love being part of the discipleship process." Another admitted feeling pressure to "prove" that true discipleship was happening in this loosey-goosey, organic way of doing small groups. The burden of feeling responsible for people's spiritual growth is not to be taken lightly. The highly regimented, control-based approach of some models has appeal, especially for leaders. Those kinds of small groups, however, will only work for the people who are at the place on their spiritual journey where they'll commit to them.

There's no doubt about it: Organic small groups can be frustrating, but then *all* small groups can be. What's more important is that they can also lead to life transformation.

Pastors aren't expected to lead perfectly. None of us is perfect, not even senior pastors (though some people think they should be). When pastors extend grace and forgiveness to others, they also receive grace and forgiveness. Grace and truth must always be held in healthy tension; of course, one at the expense of the other is a distortion of the gospel.

Servant leadership also doesn't mean that pastors have no agenda. They do. But they're willing to look to the larger picture of what God is doing with them and with their congregation, and begin to discern when one part of the body needs to be lifted up, or another needs to be nurtured and supported, or another needs to be expressed. Pastors work together with other leaders in a truth-giving, supportive, dynamic atmosphere. It's a radically different vision of leadership today, one that leads to the image in Ezekiel 43 of the river of life flowing from the temple. It's life-giving leadership that produces spiritual growth. It frees the Spirit to work, no matter who has the biggest ministry or the most resources. It honors where God is at work and joins Him there.

Pastors do well to let love lead the way. *People know when they're loved.* Though sometimes people have baggage that they drag around from their past, baggage that hinders their ability to receive love, it's still a powerful motivator. This is what God intends: "By this all men will know that you are my disciples, if you love one another" (John 13:35).

Loving God, loving one another, and loving our neighbor are biblical commands, *relational* commands. Growing people through small groups honors those commands and leads people one step at a time to becoming all that God intends, new creations in Christ enjoying the bounties of His love.

Summary Questions

1. If you're a pastor, how would you rate yourself on a scale of 1 to 10, with 1 being "very controlling" and 10 being "very empowering"? How do you think your staff or volunteer leaders would rate you?

2. If you're a paid staff or volunteer church leader, how would you rate your pastor? How would you rate yourself?

3. What issues might keep a pastor from becoming an empowering servant leader?

4. What steps could be taken to address those issues?

5. What would your church look like if it implemented the kind of leadership described in this chapter? What can you do to help begin that process of change?

AFTERWORD

By now you've probably discovered that each of the small-group stories in this book illustrates more than one idea or principle. This overlap is inevitable. Like the people in them, small groups are complex and ever-changing, and because they're organic, they're fluid and flexible in nature. Again, sometimes they're frustrating, which grows and strengthens us because it keeps our eyes focused on God.

We haven't tried to exhaust every possibility for how God grows people through small groups—our goal has been to share a strategy and some stories to show that He does. We hope our stories have sparked creativity in you; you might add stories of your own, as well as new ways that you see God working.

We've enjoyed sharing how God has shaped and changed each of us personally as we've grown on our own spiritual journey in small groups. The concepts in this book are borne of our own observations, study, and experiences as well as what we've learned from others. Our hope is that they've likewise helped you grow as a leader.

Thank you for allowing us to share what we see God doing through small groups. Going with Him on the adventure of growing people is an awesome privilege and a continuous process. He is the Originator and Director of all spiritual transformation in our lives; we simply participate with the Holy Spirit in discerning how to create an atmosphere for growth in each individual and each group. We invite you to join the adventure with us . . . and be sure you anticipate a blessing!

Supportive leadership training is available for small-group leaders and managers/coaches who are interested in the ideas in this book. Contact information is found in the Resources on the next page.

—∾—

Church's Mission & Vision

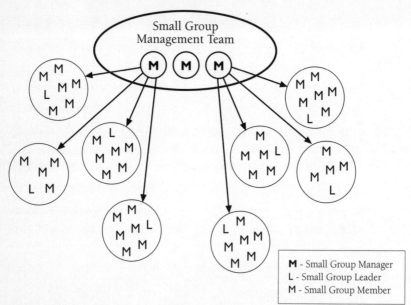

M - Small Group Manager
L - Small Group Leader
M - Small Group Member

- Each member is connected to a small group leader
- Each small group leader is connected to a manager
- The management team is connected to the church's mission and vision
- Each manager cares for no more than five small group leaders

RESOURCES

Blackaby, Henry. *Experiencing God*. Nashville: Broadman & Holman, 2003.

Coleman, Lyman. *Serendipity*. Serendipity House, 1962 (*www.serendipityhouse.com/resources*)

Collins, Jim. *Good to Great: Why Some Companies Make the Leap . . . and Others Don't*. New York: HarperCollins, 2001.

Easum, Bandy, and Associates: *www.easumbandy.com*

Kise, Jane A.G., David Stark, and Sandra Krebs Hirsh. *LifeKeys*. Minneapolis: Bethany House, 1996 (*www.bethanyhouse.com*)

Leadership Network: *www.leadnet.org*

Lencioni, Patrick. *The Five Dysfunctions of a Team*. San Francisco: Jossey-Bass, 2002.

Putnam, Robert. *Bowling Alone: The Collapse and Revival of American Community*. New York: Simon & Schuster, 2001.

Stark, David, and Patrick Keifert. *Launch and Lead Your Own Small Group*. Faith Alive Christian Resources, 2002 (*www.faithalivechristianresources.org*)

Stark, David, and Judy Stack-Nelson. *Next Steps for Small-Group Growth*. Faith Alive Christian Resources (*www.faithalivechristianresources.org*)

Vander Griend, Alvin J. *Discover Your Gifts*. Faith Alive Christian Resources, 1996 (*www.faithalivechristianresources.org*)

Warren, Rick. *The Purpose-Driven Life*. Grand Rapids: Zondervan, 2002.

Watters, Ethan. *Urban Tribes: A Generation Redefines Friendship, Family, and Commitment*. New York: Bloomsbury USA, 2003.